SPELLING
MATTERS

Bernard R. Sadler

Churchlands College of Advanced Education

Edward Arnold

First published in the United Kingdom 1982
by Edward Arnold (Publishers) Ltd
41 Bedford Square
London WC1B 3DQ

© B R Sadler 1981

Originally published by The Jacaranda Press 1981

ISBN 0 7131 0715 4

Printed in Hong Kong

Contents

Introduction

Spelling Matters is a flexible spelling scheme designed for group or individual work. The results of the test before each section indicate whether it is necessary to work through that section. The test results may be used as a basis for forming groups of students who need to work through the same section. A graph sheet is included on page 150 to record the results of the three major tests, allowing students to see the progress they have made.

The work in this book is grouped according to spelling patterns. Some rules are given after explanation, but much of the work is inductive. All spellings from the scheme are listed in the Appendix ("Word List" — page 121) with mention of the section in which each word appears. Reference to the appropriate section can thus be made in the case of specific spelling difficulties.

Many students suffer spelling disability because they lack an effective spelling learning method and simply look at words to learn their spellings. A simple but proven method of word attack is given on page ix, together with an outline of the *Word Book* to be kept by students. The *Word Book* is an important part of the scheme; misspelt words from general work should be entered as well as those words misspelt in the tests in *Spelling Matters*. Through the *Word Book*, essential revision of learning is achieved.

The etymological information placed within alternate sections provides interest, aids some spelling through knowledge of causes, and can help to stimulate inquisitiveness about language generally.

A note to students

Before you start work on this book take the "Major Spelling Test" on page 1 and enter your score on the graph at the end of the book (page 150). You will be asked to take the test again halfway through the book, and again at the end of the book. You will see your progress from the scores on the graphs.

To learn to spell a word,
1. make sure that you know how to pronounce the word;
2. break the word into syllables (a section in the book deals with this);
3. write the word without copying (cover the word if necessary);
4. write the word in your *Word Book*.

Your *Word Book*
Use a small note book. Write a letter at the top of each page — "a" on page 1, "b" on page 2 and so on.

Enter all words that you have spelt wrongly.

Ask someone to dictate four words from the book each day This is important!

Tick the words that have been dictated to you that you have spelt correctly.

Repeat the dictation exercise at intervals.

The plan
of this book

Take the "Major Spelling Test" on page 1. Graph your result on page 150.

To decide whether you need to work through a section, take the pre-test headed "Test what you know about...". Work through the sections you need, then work through the revision pages. Do each minor test — there are eight throughout the book.

Halfway through *Spelling Matters* take the "Major Spelling Test" again (page 66). Graph your result and compare it with your result on the first test to see your progress. Continue working through the sections you need. By now you will have learnt why some of our strange spellings are not so illogical after all.

Take the "Major Spelling Test" again at the end of the book (page 114). Graph your result and compare it with your previous scores to see how far you've gone on the ladders to success.

MAJOR SPELLING TEST

Insert the missing letters to complete the words in these sentences.

1. Two quarters make a half. Two h_____s make a whole.
2. It was a courag_____s act.
3. Please collect three l_____s of bread.
4. Will you write their names and ad_____s please?
5. The flies and mosq_____s were troublesome.
6. The elf gave a misch_____v_____s grin.
7. A small paper-covered booklet is a pam_____.
8. We visi_____d the island once more.
9. Our boat hap_____d to be passing.
10. We picnic_____ on the beach.
11. I off_____d to remain behind.
12. Her story dif_____d from his account.
13. The cup was accid_____y broken.
14. He read the paper critic_____y.
15. "Yours since_____y" is sometimes written at the end of a letter.
16. The tea was made aut_____ly by the machine.
17. The Indian ch_____f slowly folded his arms.
18. My nephew and my n_____ce called today.
19. What is the h_____t of that building?
20. You must forf_____t the goods you tried to smuggle.
21. Rates and tax _____ must be paid.
22. The guide replied to many enq_____.
23. "Innocent until proven g_____y" is a basic principle of our legal system.
24. Proof of payment is shown by a rec_____t.
25. After the long run he was ex_____d.

26. Keep trying and you will suc_____.
27. Please do not ex_____ the speed limit.
28. The player was transf_____d to another club.
29. The brothers quarrel_____d over the money.
30. The whole school ben_____d from the generous gift.

When you have finished the test turn to page 131 for the answers. Ask someone to check your work in case you have missed any errors. Enter any words you had wrong in your *Word Book*. Graph your result on page 150.

Time line

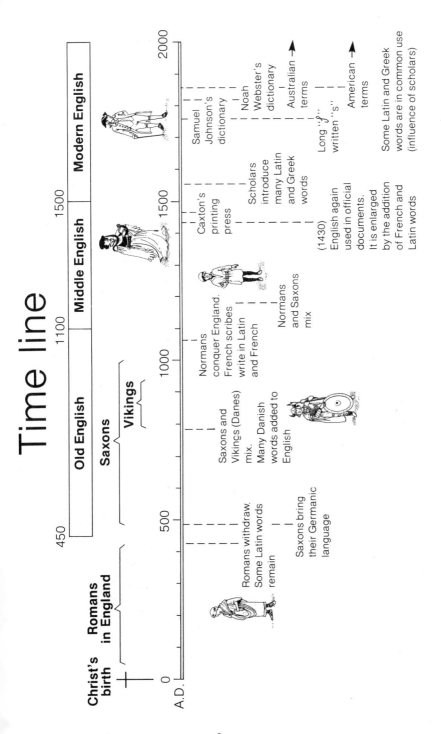

Christ's birth

Romans in England

| A.D. 0 | 500 | 1000 | 1500 | 2000 |

450 — Old English
1100 — Middle English
1500 — Modern English

Saxons
Vikings

Romans withdraw. Some Latin words remain

Saxons bring their Germanic language

Saxons and Vikings (Danes) mix. Many Danish words added to English

Normans conquer England. French scribes write in Latin and French

Normans and Saxons mix

Caxton's printing press

Scholars introduce many Latin and Greek words

(1430) English again used in official documents. It is enlarged by the addition of French and Latin words

Samuel Johnson's dictionary

Noah Webster's dictionary

Australian terms →

Long "ʃ" written "s"

American terms →

Some Latin and Greek words are in common use (influence of scholars)

3

The word "spell"

In Old English times the word "spell" meant "a story" and it came from an Old French word "espeller" which meant "to read out". It is quite easy to imagine how the word came to be used when letters of a word were read out as well as when a story was read aloud. A "reading out" also took place when magic was being attempted, and today we still use the word "spell" in connection with magic. The word "spelian" meant "substitute" in Old English times and by the Middle English period it meant "to relieve at work". Today the expression "take a spell" is sometimes used in connection with a break from work. Another word from the Old English period is "spel" meaning "news". The *good news* was the "God-spel" which we write as "gospel".

REMINDER

Do not copy a word letter by letter. See the image in your mind.

1

ROOTS

Answers begin page 135

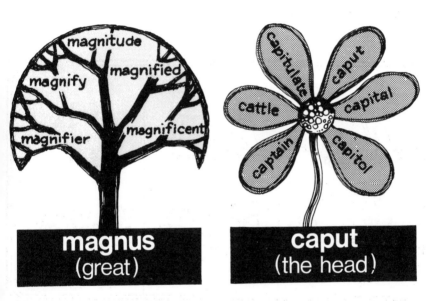

magnus
(great)

caput
(the head)

Many of the words we use come from words of another language.

We call the foreign word a *root* word. Often the word "root" is used to mean the simplest form of a word, e.g., *aqua* is the root of "aquarium".

> *ad* is a Latin word meaning "to"
> *tract* is from a Latin word meaning "to draw"
> "adtract" — to draw to — became "attract"

pro	*de*	*tract*
forward	away	to draw or to pull

5

Use the meanings of these Latin roots to find the meanings of the following words:
1. detract (the meaning may sound back to front)
2. protract

Now find the meanings of these words. The underlined roots give the meanings.
3. A <u>tract</u>or is a machine that _____.
4. A <u>tract</u>ion engine is an old machine. It also _____.

Tractable: said of a person who can be persuaded or "drawn" to do another person's desires.

Notice from the right-hand flower on page 5 that "cattle" originally meant "head".

5. Look at the drawings above. Each picture suggests a word with the Greek root *octo* in it. What are the words? Can you decide what *octo* means?
6. Several of our words come from the Latin root *tenere* which means "to hold". Over the years the pronunciation and spelling of *tenere* have changed. It still means "to hold" but it can be written as

tain   tenu   tena   tene

6

Choose from the four roots given to complete the words below:

(a) re_____ (to keep or to hold)

(b) con_____ (to hold or include)

The next two words are more difficult but they still give the idea of holding something. You will probably have to use a dictionary to complete them — simply look up the first four letters to help you find the answers.

(c) tenu_____ (holding a job)

(d) tena_____ (one who occupies property for which rent is paid)

7. The Latin root *primus* means "first". Look at the words below.

primary	primitive
prime	primeval
premier	

(a) Write each word and underline the root.

(b) A primate is a clergyman (a priest). Do you think that he has an important or unimportant job in the church? Think about the root and then write "important" or "unimportant". Write the reason for your answer.

(c) A premier works in parliament. What does the root of "premier" tell you about his job?

8. The Latin root *bene* means "good" or "well". Use a dictionary to help you find the words with the following mean-

ings. All four words begin with the root *bene*. Write the words and draw lines under the roots.

(a) benef_____: advantage or profit

(b) bene_____r: person who does good or gives money

(c) benev_____t: kindly, well-wishing

(d) bened_____: a blessing

9. "Graph" is from a Greek word meaning "write". Match each of the following words with its meaning.

(a) autograph: the story of a person's life

(b) telegraph: a line drawn to compare one value with another

(c) paragraph: a method of sending and receiving messages

(d) biography: a section of writing (in a composition, for example)

(e) graph: a signature (a written name)

10. The Latin root *gratus* means "pleasing" or "thankful". Write the following words and underline the roots. Write what each word means.

(a) grateful

(b) gratify

(c) gratitude

(d) gratuity

Base words are English words that can be made larger by the addition of prefixes and suffixes. For example, "help" is the base word of helpful, helpless and unhelpful. If you are able to spot the base word you have made the word easier to spell.

REMINDER

Base words and root words are often simply called *root words*.

8

Quiz

Use a dictionary!

Do this quiz by yourself or orally with a partner. Your partner can ask the questions and discuss the answers with you.

1. You have the following information:
   The words are from a Latin root *gratus*.
   The Latin word means "pleasing" or "thankful".

   (a) What is the root of "grateful"?
   (b) What word from the root *gratus* means a donation or a gift?
   Clue: The word has the same beginning as the Latin root. A dictionary may be used.
   (c) From the root *gratus* we have a word meaning "to satisfy". What is it?

2. You have the following information:
   The words are from a Greek root *therme*.
   The Greek word means "heat".

   (a) What is the root of the word "thermal"?
   (b) What word from the root *therme* means "an instrument to regulate heat"?
   (c) From the Greek root *therme* we have a word meaning "the science which is concerned with the changes of heat to mechanical energy". What is the word?

3. You have the following information:
   The word is from the Latin root *equus*.
   The Latin root means "horse".

   From the Latin root *equus* we have a word meaning "relating to the horse". What is the word?

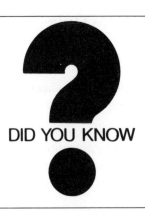

DID YOU KNOW

LATIN

According to legend, Rome was founded about two thousand years ago on the banks of the River Tiber. One of the tribes of the valley of the Tiber, the Latini, gave its name to the language which came to be used in the area.

Gradually the Romans became powerful and by the time Christ was born they ruled the world as it was known to them. Through trade and military rule many Latin words passed into the languages of nations with whom the Romans had contact. Some examples of words derived from Latin from that time are "street", "cheese" and "kitchen". The word *castra*, meaning "a fortified camp", was used of many places and can still be seen in place names ending with "caster", "chester" or "cester". Lancaster, Manchester and Cirencester are examples of such former camps.

Missionaries from Rome visited Britain in A.D. 597 and stayed to preach Christianity. We still use "priest", "nun", "abbot", "disciple", "candle", "angel", "hymn" and many other religious words derived from Latin that they introduced.

After the Norman invasion of England in the eleventh century most of the new rulers could not read or speak English. The Norman scribes probably also had little understanding of English, so they wrote government and church documents in Latin, the official language they had used in France. When, early in the fifteenth century, many writers again began to train their apprentices in the writing of English, some Latin and French words were kept. Many legal terms we use today are from Latin — "pauper", "index", "legitimate", "habeas corpus", "equivalent", "subpoena" and "affidavit" are just a few.

During the sixteenth century scholars became very interested in making translations from ancient Greek and Latin to English. Some thought that it would be a good idea to be able to recognise that an English word came from a Greek or Latin root. To do that, they made sure that the spelling of the word resembled the spelling of the Greek or Latin root, and so helped to make English spelling a little more difficult than was necessary. They put a "b" in "debt" and "doubt", an "s" in "island", a "c" in "scissors" and a "ch" in "ache". Unfortunately, the scholars were not always consistent. A "p" was inserted in "receipt", but not in "deceit".

REMINDER

Make the effort — check your spelling.

SYLLABLES

Answers begin page 136

Do you know how to split a word into syllables? If you are able to do this correctly it will be a great help in enabling you to spell unfamiliar words correctly.

It is easier to remember chunks of words, or syllables, than to remember whole words, so it seems sensible to sound the syllables in words you are trying to learn. For example:

s u p e r i n t e n d e n t

su/ per/ in/ ten/ dent

Each syllable contains a vowel sound.

Test what you know about syllables

Divide each of these words into syllables. (Notice that there may be only one syllable in the word.)

1. sit	6. manufacture
2. sitting	7. remark
3. phone	8. punctuation
4. telephone	9. necessary
5. February	10. independent

The answers are on page 136. If you have two or more errors you should work through this section. It is important that you have the correct number of syllables, although you may have split the words a little differently from the way shown.

Say these words to yourself and listen for the sounds.

    maybe   soccer   cola

Did you hear two sounds in each word?
Say the words again. Make sure that you hear the two sounds in each word.

Now write the words in syllables like this:

    may/be   soc/cer   co/la

Notice that if two consonants are together they go with different syllables — the "cc" in "soccer" is split — soc/cer. Notice how "cola" is split.

1. Write the following words in syllables. Hint: Look back at "cola" before you do word (f).

(a) manner   (e) also
(b) pencil   (f) motor
(c) appoint   (g) ladder
(d) attend   (h) local

Say the following words clearly in syllables. Sounding the words in this way will help you spell them.

athletics	horrid	tragedy	prejudice
secretary	different	interest	sandwich
environment.	government	college	quiet
thorough	through	calendar	beginning

REMINDER

Your divisions of the words may be a little different from those shown in the answers. However, you should have the same number of divisions.

---

2. Do you remember how "cola" and "motor" were. split? Write those of the following words that are split in the same way as "cola" and "motor".

    notice   lotion   written   robot
    doctor   fallen   ruler   mental

3. Look at these words:

    Āpril   sēcret   Sīmon   bōsun   dūty

13

The vowels with dashes above them stand for the same sounds as they do in the alphabet. They are long sounds.

For example: lāte   — long "a"
cūte   — long "u"
ōver   — long "o"
Pēter — long "e"
bīson — long "i"

Which of these words contain at least one long vowel?

amend   poker   silent   happy
time   rivet   sober   clip

4. Write down the words that contain at least one long vowel. Put a mark above the long vowels.

major   written   print   kind
flop   frequent   fresh   grape
gossip   rant   medium   platitude
candid   child   tuba   clan
classic   cube   custom   coconut

REMINDER

Divide double consonants.

---

5. Notice the way in which these three words are broken into syllables.

la/bour   con/duct   sit/ting

Which of the words begins with a long sound (as in ABC)?

6. Take a syllable from each column to make a three-syllable word. The first is done for you — in/stru/ment.

(a)	in	ti	pear
	mas	ap	ment
	mul	stru	cre
	dis	sa	ply

(b)	mis	ap	rate
	dis	a	rant
	sep	tau	point
	res	chie	vous

14

7. Below are syllables of words. Write the complete words with spaces to show the syllables. The first is done for you.

excel———— ——cellent ex———lent	mag————— ———azine mag-zine	occa———— ————sion oc——sion
ex cel lent		

super——tendent ———————tendent superinten————	priv————— ————ilege priv-lege

REMINDER

Split double consonants.

Divide after a long vowel, if necessary.

Separate a prefix or suffix from the base word.

---

8. There are two syllables in the word rob/ber. It has two consonants where we divide the word ("bb"), so we put one consonant with each syllable. This leaves the base word (root) whole.

Divide these words into syllables:

rotten   hopping   commerce   magnet   distance

15

9. If the root word (or base word) ends with a double consonant we do not separate the double consonant.

bless — bless/ing	bliss — bliss/ful
pass — pass/ing	small — small/est

Divide these words. Look for the root word first. If it ends with two similar letters you should keep them together as in the four words above.

chatter	fussing	hitting	fuzzy
lapping	dropping	swimmer	painter

10. Pronounce the following words in syllables and then write them in syllables:

affect	awful	athlete	elate
dispatch	calling	harass	empty
sitting	telling	tapping	falling

REMINDER

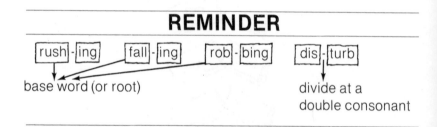

rush-ing	fall-ing	rob-bing		dis-turb

base word (or root)

divide at a
double consonant

11. A syllable can end with a long vowel as in mo/tion, but you should try to keep a consonant after a short vowel, e.g., bat/on, bal/ance.
Divide these words:

button	humble ("ble" is one syllable)
banner	pirate
radio (3 syllables)	holy
palace	notice
pilot	concentrate

12. Now divide these words of three or more syllables (sometimes called multi-syllabic). Pronounce them so that you hear the separate sounds. You may differ slightly in your

16

placement of some letters, but you should have the same number of syllables as shown in the answers.

rotation	literate
interrupt	separate
multiplication	accommodation
locomotive	successful
popular	benefit

If a word ends with "le" it is usually necessary to include the consonant before the "le", as in "cat-tle".

REMINDER

When syllabifying, split double consonants unless the base word ends with double consonants, e.g., rob/bing, tell/ing.

Try to keep the base word (or root)

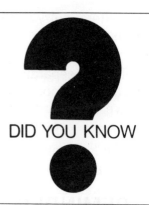

DID YOU KNOW

THE FRENCH INFLUENCE

When the Normans conquered England in the eleventh century they insisted that all official writing — regarding law, in the king's court and so on — should be in French or Latin.

Gradually some French spellings came to be used in Saxon words.

"Qu" replaced "cw". The old word for "queen" was "cwen"; the old spelling of "quick" was "cwicu".

By the fourteenth century English was again in official use, but it now included French words. Some of the "qu" words that come to us from Latin through French are quit, quest, question and quintuplet.

Have you noticed that "qu" at the end of a word makes a "k" sound and not a "cw" sound, as in cheque and antique?

Some other French or Norman words are duke, duchess, government, tax, justice, parliament, judge and prison. Do those words make you think that the Normans were rulers or workers?

REMINDER

Develop the attitude of caring about spelling.

REVISION I

Roots

The following words were introduced in the section on roots. You will doubtless find more words from the same roots.

    primary   prime   premier   primitive   primeval

    benefit   benefactor   benevolent   benediction

    octopus   October   octagon   octogenarians   octave   octet

    tenement   retain   contain   tenure   tenant

    autograph   telegraph   paragraph   biography   graph

    grateful   gratify   gratitude   gratuity

Lists of some common Greek and Latin roots are given in the Appendix on pages 116–118.

Syllables

When dividing at two consonants, split the consonants.

When dividing after a long vowel, you need not keep a consonant after the vowel.

If a word ends with "le" it is usually necessary to include the consonant before the "le".

Exception: When the word ends with "ckle"

MINOR TEST I

1. Use the words in the box to answer the questions below.

telescope	manufacture	inspire	creed	annual
audience	credit	anniversary	expire	audition

(a) Which words are from the Latin root *spiro*, meaning "I breathe"?

(b) Which word is from the Latin *manus* (the hand)?

(c) Which words are from the Latin root *credo*, meaning "I believe"?

(d) Which words are from the Latin *annus* (year)?

(e) Two words are from the Latin root *audire* (to hear). Which are they?

(f) Which word is from the Greek root *skopos* (see)?

2. Write the base words (or root words) of:

      impossibly   unusually   imprisoned   misguided

3. Syllabify these three-syllable words. It is important that you write the words in syllables.

mischievous	privilege	recommend	linguistic
interfere	umbrella	tobacco	endeavour
succession	separate	quarantine	celebrate

4. Syllabify these four-syllable words:

| accessory | necessary | accommodate | amalgamate |
| affiliate | alleviate | occasional | neutrality |

5. Use your dictionary to find the roots and origin of each of these words:

| hydrant | magnify | include |
| photograph | fluid | conclude |

The anwers are on page 131. Revise the appropriate section if you have made any errors.

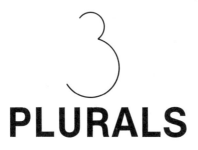

PLURALS

Answers begin page 137

Most plurals have one of two endings — "s" or "es".

Test what you know about plurals

Complete each of the following sentences by inserting the plural form of the word in brackets.

1. The two countries fought together as _____. (ally)
2. Four _____ travelled in convoy. (bus)
3. The house was supported by six _____. (column)
4. The applicants gave their names and _____. (address)
5. Students attended _____ in mathematics. (class)
6. The solicitor made _____ on behalf of his client. (enquiry)
7. Professors teach in _____. (university)
8. The _____ will be fed at four o'clock. (monkey)
9. The boy made an effort to complete his _____. (study)
10. Many people appreciate Shakespeare's _____. (tragedy)

The answers are on page 137. If you have 9 out of 10 correct you may omit this section.

We use either "s" or "es" to make plurals of most words.

Most nouns take "s" to become plural.

But these are soft sounds —

        s   ss   sh   x   ch (not when sounded "k")

— as in

        bus   witness   wish   box   lunch

If only an "s" is added to these words they are very difficult to pronounce. Try it. It is awkward, so we add "es" and we have

        buses   witnesses   wishes   boxes   lunches

This gives the following rule:

> Words with a soft ending take "es" to become plural.

Rules for words ending with "y":

> If there is a vowel before the "y" we simply add "s".

For example: delay — delays, monkey — monkeys

> If the "y" follows a consonant, we change the "y" to "i" and add "es".

For example: berry — berries, cherry — cherries

1. Make plurals of the following:
   - (a) chimney   (d) donkey
   - (b) party   (e) copy
   - (c) country   (f) journey
2. Make plurals of the words in the box and complete the sentences on the next page. Some clues are given.

country	tragedy	column	bus
study	theatre	tax	address

(a) I like to go to concert halls and _____. (t)
(b) Athletes from many _____ met in Peking. (c)
(c) _____ on the roads occur unnecessarily often. (T)
(d) Parliament increased _____. (t)
(e) _____ of men marched past the president. (C)
(f) A good student works hard at his _____. (s)
(g) Three _____ were required for the journey. (b)
(h) The _____ were indistinct and the letters were not delivered. (a)
3. Complete the sentences with plurals of the words in the box.

> reply   enquiry   valley   pitch
> property   survey   dress   university

(a) The telephonist answered many _____. (e)
(b) Several new _____ are being built. (u)
(c) From the top of the ridge we saw rivers and _____ below us. (v)
(d) Before building commenced _____ were made of the land. (s)
(e) Two country _____ were sold that day by auction. (p)
(f) Shoes, coats and _____ were on display. (d)
(g) Following the storm three cricket _____ were under water. (p)
(h) I am waiting for _____ to my letters. (r)

REMINDER

Words with a soft ending take "es", for example, wishes.

---

4. Complete each of the following sentences with the plural form of the word in brackets.
(a) Working men have to pay _____. (tax)
(b) To reach his office he had to catch two _____. (bus)
(c) Partly built _____ stood on the land. (bungalow)
(d) At the front of the building there were many ornamental _____. (arch)

25

(e) The police arrived and took names and _____.
(address)

(f) The army marched in three long _____. (column)

5. Unscramble the following words:
(a) veysurs (begins with "s")
(b) slipeer (begins with "r")
(c) heatster (begins with "t")
(d) chatsew (begins with "w")
(e) airdise (begins with "d")

6. Write the plural form of these words:

(a) party	(d) county	(g) study
(b) tragedy	(e) society	(h) property
(c) enquiry	(f) university	(i) country

7. Three words in each set of four below are misspelt. Write the correct word.
(a) discoverys   discoveries   discovries   discovereys
(b) chimneys   chimnies   chimneyes   chimneis
(c) worrys   worryes   worries   worres

REMINDER

If a word ends with a vowel and "y", add "s", for example, pulleys.

If "y" follows a consonant, change the "y" to "i" and add "es", for example, lollies.

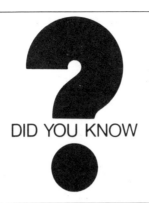

DID YOU KNOW

WORDS CHANGE IN MEANING

"Silly" originally meant "holy". A holy person is usually meek and obedient and follows instructions. The word later came to mean "not able to think sensibly and clearly".

"Handicap" is an abbreviation of "hand in the cap". Hand in the

cap was a gambling game. Items were put in a cap and players took a chance when they dipped their hands in the cap. Everyone stood an equal chance. The purpose of our modern handicap is to even the chances of all competitors.

"Nice", in its Latin form, meant "ignorant" or "inattentive". In England seven hundred years ago "nice" meant "rather foolish". Then it came to mean "fussy about small things" and later it meant "fine" or "good". Now, of course, it is a very overworked, general word meaning "pleasant".

In Old English times a "godsibb" was a god-relative — a god-mother, who was a sponsor at a baptism. The word became "gossip", which means "idle chatter" and perhaps gives a picture of two god-mothers or godsibbs of long ago.

REMINDER

Take the trouble to enter difficult words in your *Word Book*.

4
MORE DIFFICULT PLURALS

Answers begin page 138

In Old English writing, "f" was used for both hard and soft sounds, also known as voiced and voiceless sounds. We still use "f" for some hard sounds, as in the word "of". In many of our present-day nouns we change the "f" to "ve" when they become plural.

The plural of "half" is "halves". Do you know the plurals of "roof" and "thief"?

What do you add to form the plural of "radio", of "banjo" and of "potato"?

Test what you know about these more difficult plurals

Complete these sentences by inserting the plural form of the word in brackets.

1. Two _____ make a whole. (half)
2. The greenhouses were full of ripening _____. (tomato)
3. Three forks, three spoons and three _____ were on the table. (knife)
4. The shop sold television sets and _____. (radio)

To make the plural of a word ending with "o", ask if the "o" follows a consonant. If so, add "es". For example:

potato — potatoes	tomato — tomatoes
veto — vetoes	mosquito — mosquitoes
Negro — Negroes	echo — echoes

There are exceptions. To most musical words ending with "o" we simply add "s".

banjo — banjos	piano — pianos
solo — solos	piccolo — piccolos
alto — altos	canto — cantos

A few other words, rarely used in the plural, are also exceptions:

dynamo — dynamos   tobacco — tobaccos

1. Write the plurals of the following words:

echo   mosquito   piccolo   Negro
solo   tomato   hero   veto

Change "f" to "ves" to make a plural, as in
half — halves.

2. Try these:

knife   life   loaf   shelf   thief
wife   self   leaf   calf   half

Exceptions are words containing "oo", for example,
proof — proofs   roof — roofs   hoof — hoofs

30

and a few others:

safe — safes   relief — reliefs

Some dictionaries give alternative spellings for a few words, for example, handkerchiefs/handkerchieves, scarfs/scarves, hoofs/hooves, but the easiest thing to do is to follow the rules above.

3. Use the words in the box to complete the sentences.

shelves	zoos	yourselves	mosquitoes
thieves	leaves	tomatoes	wives

(a) Children enjoy visiting _____. (z)
(b) The _____ were ready for picking. (t)
(c) Expensive books were displayed on _____. (s)
(d) You must attend to these matters _____. (y)
(e) _____ withered in the drought. (L)
(f) The men and their _____ attended the conference. (w)
(g) Flies and _____ tormented the men. (m)
(h) At night _____ broke into the flat. (t)

4. Use the words in the box to complete these sentences.

mottoes	echoes	calves	solos
embargoes	halves	knives	potatoes

(a) Bandits appeared, brandishing swords and _____. (k)
(b) Cows were separated from their _____ at the sale. (c)
(c) The trumpets' _____ could be heard far away. (e)
(d) The blight affected the growth of the _____. (p)
(e) _____ were placed on trade between the two countries. (E)
(f) The apples were divided into _____. (h)
(g) Above the doorways _____ were displayed. (m)
(h) The singing of duets followed the singing of _____. (s)

REMINDER

"See" the word in your mind. Do not copy letter by letter.

5. Complete the following sentences by inserting the plural form of the word in brackets.
   (a) At night _____ worked in gangs. (thief)
   (b) Men appeared, wearing _____ on their hips. (knife)
   (c) I like visiting _____. (zoo)
   (d) _____ thrive in hot climates. (Mosquito)
   (e) Many gardeners grow their own _____ and _____.
       (potato, tomato)
   (f) Music was played on _____ and _____, and
       _____ and _____ sang _____. (piano, banjo,
       soprano, contralto, solo)
6. Unscramble the following words:
   (a) sheore (begins with "h")
   (b) sofor (begins with "r")
   (c) enregos (begins with "N")
   (d) orsegac (begins with "c")
   (e) valese (begins with "l")
   (f) soapin (begins with "p")
7. Write the plural form of these words:
   (a) wolf   (c) shelf   (e) leaf
   (b) half   (d) thief   (f) yourself
8. Write the singular form of each of these plural words:
   (a) tomatoes   (c) Negroes   (e) pianos
   (b) potatoes   (d) radios   (f) photos
9. Three words in each set of four below are misspelt. Write the correct word.
   (a) soloes   solos   solows   sowlos
   (b) vetos   vetows   vetoes   veetos
   (c) enquirys enquires enquireys enquiries
   (d) addresess addressies addresses adresses
   (e) radios   radioes radiose   radiows
   (f) loavs   loafs   loaves   loafes

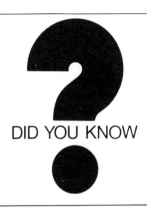

DID YOU KNOW

SILENT LETTERS

Long ago people wrote words as they said them. The word "night" used to be said with a "k" sound for the "gh". Listen to a Scot or a German say "night".

Other words such as "might" and "though" were also pronounced with the hard "k" sound. The way that the words were pronounced changed but the spelling changed very little.

...and don't drop your k's when you speak.

 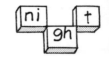

A thousand years ago, people pronounced the "k" in "knife". They also pronounced the "k" sound in "knot", "know" and "knee" and the "g" sound in "gnaw". Even when it was no longer fashionable to say "k-nife", "k-now" or "k-nee" the "k" was still written and so was called a silent letter.

When you say "hour", "honour" or "honest" you should not pronounce the "h". That is because those words were originally French. Like many French words they were taken from Latin. "Heir" and "heirloom" are also French words and each has a silent "h".

REMINDER

Do you check your guesses when spelling?

REVISION II

To form plurals

- of most nouns we simply add "s".
- of nouns with a soft ending we add "es".
- of words ending with "y"
  (i) with a vowel before the "y" we add "s" (key — keys).
  (ii) with a consonant before the "y" we change the "y" to "i" and add "es" (biography — biographies).
- of words ending with "o"
  (i) to most musical words ending with "o" we add "s" (solo — solos).
  (ii) when the "o" follows a consonant we add "es" (tomato — tomatoes).
  Exceptions are words which are rarely spelt in the plural.
- of words ending with "f" we change the "f" to "ves" to make a plural.
  Exceptions are words containing "oo" (but we can write "hoofs" or "hooves").

The following plurals were introduced in the two sections on plurals:

addresses	contraltos	handkerchieves	pianos
allies	copies	heroes	piccolos
altos	counties	hoofs	pitches
arches	countries	hooves	potatoes
banjos	dairies	journeys	proofs
berries	delays	knives	properties
boxes	discoveries	leaves	radios
bungalows	donkeys	lives	reliefs
buses	dresses	loaves	replies
calves	dynamos	loaves	roofs
cantos	echoes	lunches	safes
cargoes	embargoes	monkeys	scarfs
cherries	enquiries	mosquitoes	scarves
chimneys	fishes	mottoes	selves
classes	halves	Negroes	shelves
columns	handkerchiefs	parties	societies
		photos	

solos	thieves	vetoes	worries
sopranos	tobaccos	watches	yourselves
studies	tomatoes	wishes	zeros
surveys	tragedies	witnesses	zoos
taxes	universities	wives	
theatres	valleys	wolves	

MINOR TEST II

1. Add one of the endings to each word part to make a plural.
Write the words in your *Word Book*. (Some of the endings will
not be used.)

t	h	i	e			
p	o	t	a	t		
p	i	a	n			
m	o	s	q	u	i	t
l	e	a				
c	a	l				
t	o	m	a	t		
r	o	o				

fs
ves
ves
fs
oes
os
oes
ves
ves
oes

2. Add one of the endings to each of the word parts given. Write the words in your *Word Book*. (Not all the endings will be used.)

t	r	a	g	e	d
b	u	s			
p	r	o	p	e	r	t
d	e	l	ā		
u	n	i	v	e	r	s	i	t
s	t	u	d		

ies
ies
es
es
ys
es
ss
ies
ies

The answers are on page 132. Revise the appropriate section if you have made any errors.

HOMONYMS

Answers begin page 139

Do you know the difference between "stationery" and "stationary", between "compliment" and "complement" and other tricky pairs of words that sound the same?

Test what you know about homonyms

Complete the words in these sentences. Some clues are given to help you.

1. The driver pas_____ beautiful scenery. (went by)
2. Something rough in texture is said to be c_____rse.
3. The men were paid th_____ wages. (rhymes with "chair")
4. More prac_____ will result in great improvement.
5. The meeting was form_____ opened by the Chairman.
6. She is a lady of high prin_____.
7. The bracelet was lost because the catch was lo_____. (not tight)
8. They danced al_____gether in the ballroom.
9. I hear that it_____ still raining. (it is)
10. A new supply of sta_____ was delivered to the office. (paper)

The answers are on page 139. If you have 9 out of 10 correct you may omit this section.

Homonyms are words that are pronounced alike but spelt differently.

You probably know the difference between "whole" and "hole" and between "birth" and "berth". Are you sure of the difference between "stationary" and "stationery"?

Remember, a stationer sells paper.
When a car is stationary it is still.

Here is one way of remembering whether the following words have "i" or "e".

Compliment — I like compliments.
Complement — Everything is included in the complement.

"Complement" and "complete" are both from the Latin root complere. Notice the likeness in spelling. "Complement" is used in this way:

The ship's complement was 200 men.

Word associations such as these are helpful in remembering spellings. The best aids are those you invent yourself.

Invent your own aids for the words you have wrong on the following pages. For example:

Turn the turf and bury it.
Kerry was a berry and cherry picker.

REMINDER

Do you check a word in the dictionary if you are uncertain of its meaning or spelling?

1. Match a word from the box with the appropriate clue or definition. Write each word as a whole. Do not copy letter by letter.

principal	stationary	past	loose
weather	formerly	altogether	compliment
course	alter	their	practice

(a) Not moving (s)
(b) Completely and without exception (a)

39

(c) Time gone (p)
(d) To praise or comment favourably (c)
(e) If it belongs to them it is _____ property. (t)
(f) To make different (a)
(g) Previously (f)
(h) Not tight (l)
(i) _____ makes perfect. (P)
(j) Atmospheric conditions (w)
(k) Head of an educational institution (p)
(l) A correspondence _____ (c)

2. Match a word from the box with the appropriate clue or definition. Write each word as a whole.

coarse	whether	all together	practise
formally	complement	principle	passed
stationery	lose	altar	there

(a) A table used in religious services (a)
(b) Writing paper, envelopes, etc. (s)
(c) Fundamental rule (p)
(d) Everyone in a group (a)
(e) Past tense of "to pass" (p)
(f) Rough and uneven (c)
(g) The full ship's _____ assembled on deck. (c)
(h) Here and _____ (t)
(i) In a formal manner (f)
(j) To mislay (l)
(k) _____ your tennis. (P)
(l) Let me know _____ you will attend. (w)

Here are some more tricky pairs of homonyms, and word associations to help you remember them.

Their — there:
"Their" means "belonging to them".

"There" means place. Associate it with other place words such as "here" and "where". If you have trouble with these two words you should make up a sentence or phrase containing all three words. For example, here, there, and everywhere.

Principle — principal:

A principle is a general truth. "Principal" means the first or the most important.

The most important person in a school or college is the principal. Remember your pal the principal.

The principal reason is the most important reason.

Its — it's:

An apostrophe is *not* used in "its" to show ownership. For example:

The sun was at *its* highest.

If you wish to write the two words "it is" you may shorten them to "it's". The apostrophe shows that a letter has been omitted. For example:

The signs are that *it's* going to be a hot day tomorrow.

Gorilla — guerilla:

A gorilla is a large ape.

A guerilla is a member of an armed band that makes war behind enemy lines. The word is from the Spanish words "guerra", meaning "war", and "guerrilla", meaning "little war".

The spelling of guerilla is optional but it may help your spelling if you write both gorilla and guerilla with one "r".

Advise — advice:

The verb — the doing thing — has an "s":

"I advise you to raise your hands."
╲doing — the act of telling

The noun has a "c" (you may also notice that there is a noun within the word — advice):

"I gave him sound advice."
noun

The words "device" and "devise" follow the same rule. Where English/Australian spelling is taught, "practice" and "practise" also follow the rule. Remember, the word containing "ice" is a noun.

Passed — past:

"Passed" (verb) is a doing word (it has a "d" for doing):

      She passed the wine.   He passed the shop.
          doing   doing
      She passed the examination.

"Past" (noun, adjective, adverb) can be used in several ways but *not* as a doing word:

      He walked past the shop.
         doing
      He went past the shop.

3. Check your understanding. Complete the following sentences by using one of the words in brackets.

  (a) Dr Bleet has a large _____. (practice, practise)

  (b) The regiment marched _____ the general. (passed, past)

  (c) Ten boats _____ the finishing line. (passed, past)

  (d) You must _____ your singing. (practice, practise)

  (e) She gave me good _____. (advise, advice)

  (f) The two old soldiers talked about _____ battles. (passed, past)

42

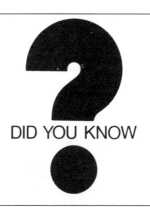

DID YOU KNOW

THE VIKING INFLUENCE

The Vikings from Norway and Denmark made many raids on England before the Norman conquest, often in great fleets of several hundred ships. King Alfred prevented the raiders from conquering the whole of England but the Danes settled in the north and east of England.

The Danes and Anglo-Saxons spoke related languages and so could understand each other quite well. After a time there was intermarriage between Danes and Anglo-Saxons. The language used by the Vikings gradually died out but we still use many of their words. Even today the dialect of people who live in the north of England differs from that of southern dwellers.

The Danes used hard sounds such as "k" more than the Saxons did. The Saxons called a short garment a "shirt", the Danes called it a "skirt" and the names now mean different things. Saxons said "church" and the Danes said "kirk". The Saxon "shrub" was the

43

Danish "scrub" and they now mean different forms of vegetation.

Bank, birth, crook, dirt, egg, gap, leg, root, scold, score, scrap, ship, sky, steak, them and their are just a few of the old Danish Viking words that we regularly use. Towns or cities whose names end with "by" or "thorpe" are reminders of the Viking influence on the English language. Derby and Stanthorpe are such towns.

REMINDER

When learning a word use the "look, cover, write" strategy.

DOUBLE LETTERS

Answers begin page 139

Test what you know about double letters

Write correctly the underlined words from the sentences below. Some underlined words are incomplete and others are spelt phonically (by sound). Not all answers contain double letters.

1. An officer holds a <u>comishun</u>.
2. Somewhere to stay or sleep is <u>ackomodayshun</u>.
3. I <u>opows</u> the idea.
4. This is an important <u>okayshun</u>.
5. That is not <u>nesesaree</u>.
6. Please wait <u>unt___l</u> come back.
7. The group was a great <u>suckses</u>.
8. The craftsman was very <u>sk_____l</u>.
9. Leave him alone. Do not <u>h___r___s</u> him.
10. The accident <u>oc___r___d</u> at sunset.

The answers are on page 139. If you have 9 out of 10 correct, you may omit this section.

Here are some guides to dealing with certain tricky spellings.

In many words we double a consonant in order to keep a vowel short. This is explained in section 10, "Long and short vowel sounds".

necessary — use a double "s" to avoid an "ee" sound in the middle.

45

occasion — note that we use one "s" to keep the "ay" sound. The wrong spelling, "occassion", must be pronounced "oh cash/un" (rhymes with "passion").

In some words we drop an "l". For example, we write only one "l" when the word "full" is part of another word (usually, but not always, an adjective).

mindful	hopeful
beautiful	joyful
helpful	skilful
handful	needful

Note: Americans sensibly keep the "ll" in the middle of skilful.

Some other words that end with one "l" are

until	dispel
quarrel	instil

appear ⎫
appoint ⎬ These three words must each have a double "p". With one "p" they would be pronounced "ay pear", "ay point", "oh pose".
oppose ⎭

An exception to the general rule is "harass". Note that this word has only one "r".

1. Use the words in the box to complete the sentences below. When writing the words try to remember them as whole words or whole syllables. Do not copy letter by letter. Underline the double letters in the words you use.

success	access	traffic	occurred	parallel
quarrel	omitted	account	accuse	beginning

(a) Two equidistant lines are p_____l.
(b) To disagree angrily is to qu_____l.
(c) The opposite of failure is s_____s.
(d) To gain admittance is to have ac_____s.
(e) The start is the beg_____g.
(f) A reckoning is an ac_____nt.
(g) To blame is to ac_____se.
(h) Om_____ted means missed out.

(i) Tr_____ic is a term used for vehicles on roads.

(j) Something that has happened has oc_____d.

2. Each of the following words has the letters "acc" missing. Write each word in full, matching it with the correct definition. The definitions are given below the words.

(a) -use	(f) -ompany
(b) -ount	(g) -ommodation
(c) -ost	(h) -limatise
(d) -ouchement	(i) -elerate
(e) -omplish	(j) -umulate

To collect or increase

To go with a person

Somewhere to live

To increase speed

To charge with wrong-doing

A record or a reckoning

To become used to a climate

To achieve something

To speak to a stranger in a familiar or rude way

The childbirth period

Write "accommodation". Underline the double letters as shown.

Write "embarrass". Draw lines under the double letters.

Write "assassin". Underline the double letters.

Write "success". Show the double letters by underlining.

Write "access". Draw lines under the double letters.

Write "commission". Draw lines under the double letters.

Here are the six words again:

accommodation

embarrass

assassin

success

access

commission

Enter the list in your *Word Book*. You might like to add other words such as balloon and succeed.

Association of several of the words might help you to remember them. For example: "It occurred to me that I would have success in finding accommodation."

47

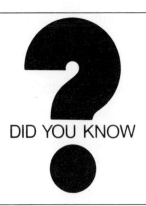

DID YOU KNOW

EARLY PRINTING

The first printing press to be used in England was introduced by William Caxton in 1476. Although the press was crude, it was, of course, capable of producing books at a much greater rate than scribes could write them by hand. The Saxon scribes wrote some words as people pronounced them in their locality, but as they usually made only a few copies of each book that did not matter.

Printed books were sent all over England and readers began to accept the spellings in the books as the correct way to spell. Standardisation of spelling took a long time, however, and even in the 1600s some words might be spelt differently in the same book, particularly if more than one compositor had worked on the book.

Caxton had spent much of his life in the Netherlands and he employed Dutch craftsmen to operate his press. Some of our present-day spellings date back to that time. The craftsmen used the Dutch "gh" spelling to represent "g" and we still write "ghost" and "ghastly", whereas before printed books the normal spellings were "gast" (spirit) and "gastlic" (terrible).

Unfortunately, printing was introduced at about the time that speech was changing. Printers continued to write words as they had once been pronounced, and we still write the "l" in "should" and "would" even though it ceased to be pronounced long ago. Another change in spoken English was the dropping of many word endings — "comman" became "come", "habben" became "have" and "lifan" became "live". The word ending was dropped but an "e" was added even though our spelling of the words might be easier without that "e".

An "e" was added to many words without good reason. Have you seen the old spellings "Inne" and "Shoppe"?

By 1700, spelling was much as we know it today. It is strange to think that by the year 1000 the Anglo-Saxons had agreed on a standard way to spell many words. The Norman invasion of England upset what had promised to be a very stable system of spelling.

REMINDER

Break a long word into syllables.

REVISION III

Homonyms

Practice or practise? Device or devise? Remember that the noun has the noun "ice" in it.

The doctor has a large pract*ice*. (a noun)

The doctor will practise here. (a verb, because it is something he will do)

The dev*ice* worked well. (a noun)

We must devise a better way. (a verb, because it is something we must do)

Prophecy or prophesy? Licence or license? The above rule helps with these words too. The words with "c" are nouns.

"Prophecy" is a noun. "Prophesy" is a verb.
"Licence" is a noun. "License" is a verb.

Its or it's? The apostrophe is only used after "it" to indicate that a letter is missing. "It's" is short for "it is".

Princi*pal* means first or most important. For example: The excellent photography was the princi*pal* reason for the film's success.

Double letters

Remember the two sets of double letters in the following words:

accommodation	embarrass	access
success	assassin	commission

Plurals

To form plurals of words that end with "y":

add "s" if the "y" follows a vowel, e.g. donkey — donkeys;

if the "y" follows a consonant, change the "y" to "i" and add "es".

MINOR TEST III

1 (a) Write the nouns among the words below:

        practice   practise   advise
        advice   prophesy prophecy

  (b) How can the nouns (names) be distinguished from the verbs (the action words)?

2. Complete the following sentences:
  (a) She p_____ the driving test. (pass)
  (b) The car was station_____.
  (c) This is our house and that is th_____ house. (their/there)
  (d) The cloth is very c_____rse. (rough)
  (e) We must alt_____ those figures. (change)

3. Rewrite the following sentences with correct spelling:
  (a) The books on the shelvs helped with her studys of monkeys.
  (b) Thank you for your enquirys about the propertys we have for sale.

4 (a) More than one class: clas_____
  (b) More than one monkey: monk_____
  (c) More than one bus: bus_____
  (d) More than one tragedy: traged_____
  (e) More than one copy: cop_____
  (f) More than one journey: journ_____

The answers are on page 132. Revise the appropriate chapter, or chapters, if you have made any errors.

7
WORD ENDINGS — "LY" AND "ALLY"

Answers begin page 140

Test what you know about these word endings

Complete these sentences by finishing the base word (shown in brackets). You must add "ly" or "ally". You may have to modify the spelling of the base word.

1. To avoid error the loose change was examined _____ . (critic)
2. I am _____ awake by 6 a.m. (usual)
3. A repeating pistol fires _____ . (automatic)
4. That isn't _____ true. (entire)
5. He _____ put on his raincoat before leaving. (sensible)
6. I'll _____ come if I'm allowed. (certain)
7. When asking forgiveness, I speak _____ . (apologetic)
8. If it is likely to happen it _____ will. (probable)
9. The police were _____ informed of the intended bank raid. (reliable)
10. The ship was _____ holed. (accident)

The answers are on page 140. If you have 9 out of 10 correct, you may omit this section.

Most words with "ly" or "ally" endings are adverbs. The most usual ending is "ly". Add "ally" if the word ends with "ic". For example:

$$usual \longrightarrow usually$$
$$accidental \longrightarrow accidentally$$
$$automatic \longrightarrow automatically$$
$$basic \longrightarrow basically$$

1. Make these words into adverbs:

> equal
> critic
> academic
> natural

Keep an "e" when it does some work. Otherwise, drop a silent "e" before an "ly" ending.

> severe ("e" needed — not "sever") $\longrightarrow$ severely
> entire ("e" needed — not "entir") $\longrightarrow$ entirely
> irritable (silent "e") $\longrightarrow$ irritably

2. Add "ly" endings to these words:

> sincere
> sensible
> simple
> rare

When the word has a "y" ending, change the "y" to "i" and add "ly". For example:

$$funny \longrightarrow funn-i-ly$$
$$temporary \longrightarrow temporar-i-ly$$

There are a few exceptions — coyly, slyly, shyly, wryly.

3. Try these.
   (a) Write the adverbs from the following words:

> noisy   messy
> easy   happy

   (b) Write the following words as adjectives, e.g., tidily — tidy:

> wearily   lazily
> crazily   warily

REMINDER

Add "ally" to words ending with "ic". Exception: public — publicly.

4. Add "ly" or "ally" endings to the words in the box to complete the sentences following. To help you understand the rule, write explanations. If you simply add "ly", write "ly" after you have written the answer. Write "ic" if that is why you added "ally".

sensible	usual	critical	drastic	basic
probable	public	automatic	entire	certain

(a) The doors opened _____. (a)
(b) We _____ eat at 8 o'clock. (u)
(c) He _____ announced his intention to stand for parliament. (p)
(d) Eat _____ and keep healthy. (s)
(e) We agree _____ with the decision. (e)
(f) His income was _____ cut. (d)
(g) Bread is made _____ of flour and water. (b)
(h) Two people were _____ injured. (cr)
(i) We will _____ spend our holidays in the south. (p)
(j) I missed the last meeting but will _____ attend the next. (c)

5. Add "ly" or "ally" endings to the words in the box to complete the sentences. As in exercise 4, you should give an explanation of your answer.

reliable	accidental	easy	cruel	moral
simple	apologetic	severe	fundamental	equal

(a) He was _____ opposed to drilling for oil in the National Park. (f)
(b) His action was _____ wrong. (m)
(c) The speaker was _____ criticized. (se)

54

(d) She made her excuse _____. (a)

(e) The land was divided _____. (e)

(f) The children were _____ and neatly dressed. (s)

(g) He _____ beat the other competitors. (e)

(h) In zoos animals are sometimes treated _____. (c)

(i) The story was _____ reported to the newspaper. (r)

(j) The child tripped and broke the cup _____. (a)

Note: Simply add "ly" to "accidental" and "fundamental". Can you see why?

6. Complete the words in italic (sloping) type in the following sentences by adding "ly" or "ally" endings.

(a) Meetings were *usual____* planned to begin at 8 o'clock.

(b) The governor *public____* announced his decision.

(c) It was *probab____* too late to correct the error.

(d) He *sensib____* agreed to defer the move.

(e) The plan was *entire____* accepted.

(f) The driver was *automatic____* banned from the race.

(g) No one was *critic____* injured.

(h) She was *basic____* a sensitive girl.

(i) The family's spending was *drastic____* reduced.

(j) The young man *apologetic____* took his seat.

7. Make two columns, one headed "ally" and the other "ly". Add the appropriate ending to each of the following words and write it under the appropriate heading.

apologetic____	critic____
usual____	drastic____
probab____	entire____
automatic____	sensib____
basic____	public____
severe____	permanent____

8. Try to unravel the following mixed-up words:

(a) relucyl (begins with "c")

(b) limyps (begins with "s")

(c) roalmyl (begins with "m")

(d) saylie (begins with "e")

(e) qaeulyl (begins with "e")

9. Write the correct spelling of these words:

awtomatiklee   sertunlee   reliablee

publiklee   drastiklee   axidentelee

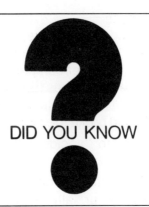

DID YOU KNOW

OLD WORDS AND NEW WORDS

Many of the words that we use today were unknown to people who lived in Victorian times. Words such as "fission" (splitting), "quasar" (one of the most distant bodies that can be seen in the sky) and "fall-out" (radioactive particles from a nuclear explosion) are scientific terms. "Espresso" and "pizza" are examples of food words from other countries that have recently come into common use in English.

"Polyester", "Terylene" and "Orlon" are names for man-made fibres. "Nylon", another trade name, comes from the location of the offices of the parent company which was based in New York and London.

As words come into usage some words go out. The word "surcease", meaning "stop" or "interval", is very rarely used nowadays. You would probably not say "crescence" if you meant "increase", or "sweb" if you meant "spoon". The Old English words "sweffen" (a dream) and "dyppan" (baptise) are not used, but we do have the word "dip" from "dyppan". Notice the endings of the Old English words.

Have you ever used "clancular", meaning "secretive", or "ataraxy", meaning "a calmness of the mind"? "Whence" means "from where" and "thence" means "from there" but these words are rarely used nowadays.

Words often die out with fashions. A "farthingale" was a petticoat spread out by hoops. "Knickerbockers" were wide breeches gathered in at the knees.

Some words are dead in normal English speech and writing, but alive in American English. "Gotten" is an example. "Fall" is an old, but more descriptive, word for autumn. "Fall" is widely used in those parts of the United States and Canada where most trees lose their leaves after they attractively and spectacularly change colour.

REMINDER

Concentrate on the troublesome part of a word.

WHICH TO USE — "EI" OR "IE"?

Answers begin page 141

Which of the above pairs of letters should go in p____ce or in l____sure?

Test what you know about these pairs of letters

Write in full the word that goes in each of these sentences. You are given some of the letters in the word.

1. The most important is the _____. (chf)
2. It was two kilograms in _____. (wt)
3. If it is from another country it is _____. (frn)
4. When we think it is true we _____ it. (blv)
5. My brother's daughter is my _____. (nc)
6. Part of it is a _____ of it. (pc)
7. To give or give up is to _____. (yld)
8. The overhead part of a room is the _____. (clng)
9. "Vanity" means the same as "_____". (cnct)
10. Ships may carry cargo, or _____. (frt)

The answers are on page 141. If you have more than one spelling wrong you should work through this section.

1. All the words in the box below contain "ei" or "ie". Say the words and write those in which the underlined letters make an "ee" sound.

neighbour	niece	vein
believe	either	field
relieve	grievance	handkerchief
weight	brief	heifer
reign	piece	chief
leisure	eight	retrieve

You can now begin to make your own rule about "ie". Here is the start. See if you can finish it:

When the sound is "ee" ....

(You will add to this rule.)

2. In all words in the box below, the "ei" or "ie" makes an "ee" sound. Sort the words into two groups under the headings "ei" and "ie".

yield	field
receive	conceive
retrieve	deceit
shriek	receipt
believe	relief

Notice which letter is before "ei". Now complete the rule you started above:

When the sound is "ee", write "i" before "e" except ....

3. Use your rule to put "ei" or "ie" in the words below.

bel--f	w--ght
rec--ve	perc--ve
dec--t	c--ling
v--n	for--gn
n--ce	gr--f

The few exceptions will be given later.

The rule you made may be something like this:

When the sound is "ee" write "i" before "e" except after "c".

Using the rule:

(a) believe

The word makes an "ee" sound, so we use the rule, "i" before "e" except after "c".

(b) receive

Does the word make an "ee" sound? Yes, so we use the rule, "i" before "e" except after "c".

(c) weight

This word does not make an "ee" sound, so the rule does not apply.

4. Look at the above and then study the incomplete words below. Decide which example applies. Write the full word and the reason for your spelling. The first one is done for you.

d e c • • t ⟶ deceit (Example (b))
    w • • g h t
r e l • • f
    p • • c e
r e c • • p t
   f r • • g h t
b e l • • v e

5. Match the words in the box with the definitions or clues following.

freight	niece	weight	foreign	deceive
relief	conceit	chief	ceiling	height

(a) To cheat (d)
(b) The most important (ch)
(c) Of another country (f)
(d) Goods transported (fr)
(e) Roof of a room (c)
(f) Not a nephew (n)
(g) A measure of how far up (h)
(h) A measure of how heavy (w)
(i) Alleviation, an easing of unpleasantness (r)
(j) A very high self-opinion (c)

60

6. Match the words in this box with the definitions or clues following.

forfeit	grievance	leisure	receive	believe
brief	shriek	alien	neighbour	perceive

(a) Cause for complaint (g)
(b) A piercing cry (s)
(c) Time for pleasure or relaxation (l)
(d) To recognize the truth of (b)
(e) Foreign (a)
(f) Short (b)
(g) Penalty (f)
(h) To see (p)
(i) To accept (r)
(j) A person who lives near (n)

7. Complete the words in the following sentences by inserting either "ei" or "ie".
(a) I do not wish to dec--ve you.
(b) The young lady's conc--t was clear to see.
(c) I hope to rec--ve a letter from you.
(d) Jane had one n--ce and one nephew.
(e) We have very pleasant n--ghbours.
(f) I offered help to rel--ve the pressure on her.
(g) Her story was difficult to bel--ve.

8. Divide the following words into two sets, those with "ei" in one column and those with "ie" in another.

fr--ght	rel--f	rec--ve
l--sure	w--ght	h--ght
for--gn	bel--f	forf--t
p--ce	--ght	ch--f

REMINDER

"I" before "e" except after "c" when it makes an "ee" sound.
Exceptions: seize, weird, caffeine.

---

9. Make a list of the correctly spelt words from those below.

grievance	cashier	yeild
conceivable	breif	thief
acheive	beleive	siege

REMINDER

Do you list the words you find troublesome?

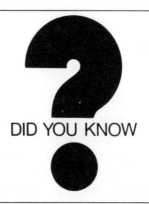

DID YOU KNOW

CONTRIBUTIONS TO ENGLISH

Many nations or peoples have contributed words to the English language. The following list shows the origins of some.

Africa: gorilla, guinea, chimpanzee

American Indians: totem, tomahawk, moccasin

Arabs: algebra, arsenal, alkali, assassin, syrup, divan

Australia: outback, bushranger, swagman, sundowners, kangaroo, billy, boomerang.

China: tea, tycoon, kowtow

Czechoslovakia: robot
Germany: masterpiece, superman, halt, swindler, blitz, dirndl
India: swastika, yoga, bungalow, juggernaut, shampoo, dinghy
France/Italy: concert, compliment, attach, cash, pilot, medal, manage, pilgrim
Japan: kimono, samurai, haiku, ju-jitsu
Malaysia: caddy
Poland: polka, mazurka
Russia: vodka, steppe, sputnik, balalaika
U.S.A.: telephone, typewriter, lynch, stunt, clearing, catfish, doughnut, jumbo, and many words to do with business and the space age

REVISION IV

Word endings — "ly" and "ally"

Add "ally" if the word ends with "ic".

Would you add "ly" or "ally" to these words?

shy	lyric	academic
hard	large	practical
basic	automatic	general

Drop the "e" at the end of a word when you add "ly" unless it does some work. For example:

savage — savagely (The "e" keeps the "g" soft.)

nice — nicely (The "e" keeps the "c" soft.)

Plurals

To make the plural of words ending with "y",

(a) add "s" if a vowel comes before the "y", for example, ray — rays;

(b) otherwise, change the "y" to "ies", for example, story — stories.

How would you change these words to plurals? (Watch for the vowel before the "y".)

monkey   jelly
berry   puppy

Simply add "s" to names, for example, "Three Marys were at the party."

Homonyms

"ise" and "ice"

Remember that the nouns contain the noun "ice" — practice (noun), practise (verb).

Here, there and everywhere — "there" means place. ("Their" means "belonging to them".)

64

MINOR TEST IV

1. Complete the words in these sentences by filling in the missing letters.
   (a) Some cars were moving but others were station____y.
   (b) The princip____ (main) reasons were stated.
   (c) The players were determined not to lo____ the game.
   (d) She drove carefully pas____ the crowd.
   (e) He rubbed it with co____se (rough) sandpaper.
   (f) Please put the luggage over th____.
   (g) Did you see the cow lick it____ calf?
2. Add one of the two word endings to the words on the left to form adverbs. If you are not sure which ending you should use, pronounce the whole word carefully.

(a)	proud_____	
(b) critic_____		**ly**
(c)	fierce_____	
(d) apologetic_____		
(e)	probab_____	
(f) drastic_____		**ally**
(g)	automatic_____	
(h) accidental_____		

3. If a word ends with "ic", do we add "ly" or "ally"?
4. Write what you would do to make plurals of words that end with "y"
   (a) where there is a vowel before the "y" (e.g. monkey), and
   (b) where there is a consonant before the "y" (e.g. lady).
The answers are on page 132. Revise the appropriate section if you have made any errors.

MAJOR SPELLING TEST

Insert the missing letters to complete the words in these sentences.

1. Two quarters make a half. Two h_____s make a whole.
2. It was a courag_____s act.
3. Please collect three l_____s of bread.
4. Will you write their names and ad_____s please?
5. The flies and mosq_____s were troublesome.
6. The elf gave a misch____v____s grin.
7. A small paper-covered booklet is a pam_____.
8. We visi_____d the island once more.
9. Our boat hap_____d to be passing.
10. We picnic_____ on the beach.
11. I off_____d to remain behind.
12. Her story dif_____d from his account.
13. The cup was accid_____y broken.
14. He read the paper critic_____y.
15. "Yours since_____y" is sometimes written at the end of a letter.
16. The tea was made aut_____ly by the machine.
17. The Indian ch_____f slowly folded his arms.
18. My nephew and my n_____ce called today.
19. What is the h_____t of that building?
20. You must forf_____t the goods you tried to smuggle.
21. Rates and tax_____ must be paid.
22. The guide replied to many enq_____.
23. "Innocent until proven g_____y" is a basic principle of our legal system.
24. Proof of payment is shown by a rec_____t.
25. After the long run he was ex_____d.
26. Keep trying and you will suc_____.

66

27. Please do not ex_____ the speed limit.
28. The player was transf_____d to another club.
29. The brothers quarrel_____d over the money.
30. The whole school ben_____d from the generous gift.

When you have finished the test turn to page 131 for the answers. Ask someone to check your work. in case you have missed any errors. Enter any words you had wrong in your *Word Book*. Graph your result on page 150.

WORD ENDINGS — "EOUS", "IOUS" and "OUS"

Answers begin page 143

Do you know which of the above endings you should use? "Danger" becomes "danger*ous*", but do you know which ending "courage", "mischief", "plenty" or "mystery" would have?

Test what you know about these word endings

Complete the following sentences by adding the missing words. You are given clues.
1. He was accused of _____ driving.
   (dang_____s)
2. The lion trainer acted in a _____ way.
   (cour_____s)
3. She had the choice of _____ colours.
   (var_____s)
4. The queen waved in a _____ manner.
   (gra_____s)
5. They enjoyed _____ exercise.
   (vig_____s)
6. He said that the council's action was _____.
   (out_____s)

68

7. The food was _____.
   (del_____s)
8. Goblins behave in a _____ fashion.
   (misch_____s)
9. The defeated boxer was soon _____ again.
   (cons_____s)
10. _____ books make me smile.
    (Hum_____s)

The answers are on page 143. If you have 9 out of 10 correct you may omit this section.

If a word ends with a consonant we simply add "ous", e.g., riot — riotous.

If a word ends with a silent "e" we drop the silent "e" before adding "ous", e.g., adventure — adventurous, ridicule — ridiculous.

Exceptions: Where the "e" is used to make "g" or "c" soft, e.g., advantage, grace.

We do not want the sounds "advantag-ous" or "grays-ous". So, to keep a "g" soft we retain the "e", e.g., advantage — advantageous, courage — courageous.

To obtain a "shus" ending we add "ious", e.g., grace — gracious.

With words ending with "y" we drop the "y" and add "eous" or "ious". Most words take "ious":

glory — glorious   fury — furious
injury — injurious   mystery — mysterious
study — studious   victory — victorious

The words that need to keep a strong "ee" sound take "eous":

bounty — bounteous
beauty — beauteous
plenty — plenteous

You will find it easier to remember such words if you exaggerate the pronunciation — "bount-ee-ous".

69

We change a final "f" to "v" when adding "ous", e.g., mischief — mischievous, grief — grievous.
Note: "ous" only is added.

1. Match each word in the box with one of the definitions following.

spacious	dangerous	mysterious	mischievous
courageous	ridiculous	various	gracious
grievous	outrageous		

(a) Having courage (c)
(b) Full of mystery (m)
(c) Absurd (r)
(d) Tending to stir up trouble (m)
(e) Abusive, offensive (o)
(f) Warm in manner, courteous (g)
(g) Having space (s)
(h) Assorted (v)
(i) Hazardous, unsafe (d)
(j) Harmful, severe (g)

2. Match the words in the box with their definitions.

obvious	conscious	ferocious	obnoxious
plenteous	serious	advantageous	mountainous
delicious	religious		

(a) Tasty (d)
(b) Clear (o)
(c) Grave, solemn (s)
(d) Abundant (p)
(e) Offensive, annoying (o)
(f) Fierce, savage (f)
(g) Pious, devout (r)
(h) In full possession of one's senses (c)
(i) Having many mountains (m)
(j) Beneficial (a)

3. Sort the following words into two groups, those with "eous" endings in one column and those with "ious" endings in another.

obvious	bounteous	outrageous
courageous	gorgeous	plenteous
mysterious	various	spacious
advantageous	religious	conscious
ferocious	piteous	obnoxious

Now cover Question 3 and work Questions 4 to 7.

4. Add "ous" to the following words. Alter or drop the last consonant where necessary.

space	outrage
courage	mystery
grief	vary
danger	mischief
ridicule	grace

5. Complete the following sentences:
   (a) The house had many rooms and felt airy and spa_____s.
   (b) There was a deli_____s smell coming from the kitchen.
   (c) In the cellar there was an obnox_____s smell.
   (d) His face showed that he thought it was outrag_____s.
   (e) The stain on the tablecloth was obv_____s.
   (f) The drawer contained shirts of var_____s sizes.

6. Insert the missing letters in the following words:

   misch____v____s   mount____n____s   grac____s
   ridic____l____s   gr____v____s   obv____s
   c____rag____s   d____ng__ r____s   relig____s

7. Write the answers to the following clues:
   (a) A word meaning courteous, pleasant and warm in manner: grac_____
   (b) A word meaning moderate in eating and drinking: abstem_____
   (c) Another word for not frank: dev_____
   (d) A word meaning devoted to study: stud_____
   (e) Another word for assorted: var_____

71

(f) A word meaning premature or former: prev_____

(g) Another word for grave or solemn: ser_____

These words must have the American spelling "or" before the suffixes:

vigour — vigorous
humour — humorous
rigour — rigorous
odour — odorous

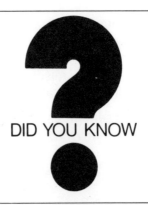

DID YOU KNOW

Oddities

Can you make a "kh" sound? Try it. The Anglo-Saxons used such a sound and spelt it with an "h". The Normans did not have this sound in their language and changed the spelling to "gh" when they wrote the words "ought", "fought", "neighbour". As the years passed, the English omitted the "kh" sound from such words but kept the Norman spelling. If you say the words with the "kh" sound you will have a rough idea of the way they were spoken a thousand years ago.

"Hymn" and "autumn" are words that come from the Latin words *hymnus* and *autumnus*. In time the words changed so that the last syllable "nus" was not pronounced. However, the "n" was kept in the spelling of the words and reminds us of their origin.

At the beginning of the eleventh century Old English scribes used either "i" or "y" in words. We still use some words that can be spelt with either letter — gipsy/gypsy, pigmy/pygmy, siren/syren. Some English-speaking countries write of a car "tyre" and others write of a car "tire". ("Tire" also means "to weary", of course.) In the seventeenth century the custom developed of using "i" at the beginning and in the middle of words. "Y" was used at the ends of words, for example, duty — dutifully.

Two "i's" were not written together — "dying", not "diing".

y to i

lyft lift describe descryve pyty pity
white whyte wych witch myght might
dayely daily cyng king
forgyve forgive
synging singing
happy happiness
dry drier
fly flies

LONG AND SHORT VOWEL SOUNDS

Answers begin page 144

Do you know the difference between "hoping" and "hopping"? Do you know whether to write "writting" or "writing"? Were you "pipped" or "piped" at the post?

Test what you know about long and short vowel sounds

Complete the following sentences with the correct form of the word in brackets.

1. Samuel Johnson spent seven years _____ his dictionary. (write)
2. The frog was _____ towards the lake. (hop)
3. He _____ the notice to the board yesterday. (pin)
4. Do you like fresh or _____ pineapple? (can)
5. The fruit will soon _____. (ripe)
6. The carpenter _____ the wood smooth. (plane)
7. Have you _____ in reply? (write)
8. James is _____ than John. (fit)
9. The use of drugs is _____. (ban)
10. I have _____ my shirt. (rip)

The answers are on page 144. If you have 9 out of 10 correct you may omit this section.

You may remember that on page 13 long sounds were shown with a dash above the vowel like this:

māke   sēcret   līfe   ōpen   fūse

They represent the alphabet names of the vowels.

1. Some of the words below contain long vowels. Write those words and mark ⁻ over the long vowels.

> tap   tame   lock   ripe   rope
> climb   chin   check   scrub   be

Short vowels are sometimes shown like this:

măt   nĕt   fĭsh   hŏp   tŭb

2. Write each of the words below and put a mark over each vowel to show whether it is long or short. Do not put a mark over a magic (mute) "e".

> cap   cape   rat   rate   hop
> hope   slide   slid   use   us
> rob   robe   fine   fin   pane
> pan   fat   fate   stripe strip

3. Show whether the base words below have long or short vowels by putting the appropriate mark above the vowels. (Do not bother putting a mark over the "ing".)

> writing   hoping   pining   pinning
> robing   robbing   canning   caning

REMINDER

Do you proof-read your writing?

If you wish to add a suffix — "ing" or "ed" — double the last consonant to keep the vowel short. For example:

hop — hopping

4. From below choose the words with *short* vowels and add "ing". Make sure that you double the last consonant to keep the vowel short.

> pin   write   rob   pad   pipe
> cane   make   rip   line slap

5 (a) Add "ing" to the words below that have *long* vowels (do not leave "e" with "ing").

> write   sit   grate   gape   run
> slide   cut   hope   claim   pip

(b) Now give an "ed" ending to the same words, where appropriate.

6 (a) Add "ing" to each of the words below. You must decide whether you want to keep the vowel short or long.

> name   let   bet   thin   spin
> throw   bite   sag   plane   stain

(b) Now add "ed" to each of the words below. Double the final consonant where necessary.

> ram   cream   mail   rub   crop
> slip   fear   coat   seat   jail

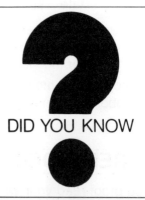

DID YOU KNOW

MORE ODDITIES

A "g" can make a hard sound, as in "gate". It can also make a soft sound, as in "gentle". Four hundred years ago printers often used the Dutch "gh" or the French "gu" to show the hard "g" sound. We still write the "gu" in "guilt", "guess", "guild" and "guard", even though the words had once been spelt "gylt", "gessan", "gild" and "garde". If you have trouble remembering how to spell "guard", remember that it has the French "gu". It may also be helpful to exaggerate the sounds and say "goo-ard".

The Anglo-Saxon word for "pray" was "biddan". People kept count of their prayers on a string on which little balls were threaded (like rosary beads). The word "bede" came to mean either the prayer or the string of balls. Gradually the word changed to mean a small ball and today our spelling is "bead". In the Middle Ages a "bedehouse" was an almshouse or hospital where the inmates prayed for those who donated money. Beadsmen or beadswomen prayed for those who gave them charity.

The Norman scribes, who often wrote in Latin, sometimes followed the Latin practice of using "o" to represent a "u" sound. Many of our present-day spellings keep the "o" — thorough, honey, love, tongue, worry and come are some examples. Can you think of others?

The use of "o" clearly showed the difference between sun/son, sum/some. The "o" prevented any confusion which might have occurred when a "u" was placed next to up-down letters such as "n" or "m". These letters were similar in early styles of writing in England.

REVISION V

Words with "ei" or "ie"

When the sound is "ee" write "i" before "e" (except after "c").
For example:

chief. The sound is "ee". It is not directly after "c", so write
"i" before "e".

(Exceptions: seize, weird, caffeine)

Words with "ous" or "eous"

To most words, add "ous". Drop the "e" at the end of most
words, e.g., adventure — adventurous.

Keep the "e" if you want a soft "c" or soft "g" sound, e.g.,
outrage — outrageous.

If the word is to have a soft ending use "ious", e.g., conscious,
ferocious, religious, delicious, contentious.

Vowel sounds

There are short vowels in words such as căt, pĕt, kĭt, dŏg and
pŭp.

To keep a vowel short when you add "ing" or "ed" you normally
double the last letter, e.g., cut — cutting.

If a silent "e" is used to indicate a long vowel you should drop it
before adding "ing", e.g., cope — coping.

MINOR TEST V

1. Complete the words in these sentences by adding "ei" or
"ie".
   (a) He stepped up to rec____ve the medal.
   (b) I bel____ve that to be the truth.

(c) This is a haunt of th____ves and vagabonds.
(d) The army laid s____ge to the castle.
(e) How would you w____gh an elephant?

2. Complete the words below with the suffix shown. You must decide whether to double the last consonant or take out any letters.

(a)	wheel	ed
(b)	write	en
(c)	place	ing

(d)	nail	ing
(e)	shop	ed
(f)	skin	ing

(g)	drum	ed
(h)	wipe	ing
(i)	begin	ing

3. Complete each of the words below by using the appropriate word ending — "ous", "ious" or "eous". Write each word in full.
(a) obv____
(b) ser____
(c) mischiev____
(d) grac____

(e) courag____
(f) consc____
(g) ridicul____
(h) myster____

(i) humor____
(j) delic____
(k) relig____
(l) spac____

Turn to page 133 for the answers. Revise the appropriate section if you have made any errors.

79

11

SILENT LETTERS

Answers begin page 144

Some words contain letters that are not sounded when the words are spoken. The letters may be in the words because they were once sounded. The pronunciations have changed but the way of writing the words has often not changed. The "rh" in "rheumatism" and "rhythm" were once sounded. If you sound the "rh" to yourself it will help you to spell "rh" words correctly.

Many words have unusual spellings because they are of foreign origin. Some words are not spelt logically because it became fashionable to indicate the origin of a word by its spelling. Samuel Johnson, who wrote an early, authoritative dictionary, inserted the "p" in "receipt" but was inconsistent and did not put it in "deceit". A "g" was mistakenly inserted in "sovereign" and "foreign" because they were wrongly associated with "reign"; there is a "g" in the original French word "regne". We cannot now discard the unnecessary "g" because printing houses and dictionary compilers use it, and they set the standards of correct usage.

Test what you know about words with silent letters

Write the answers to the clues given. Remember, each answer is a word with a silent letter.
1. Leaves fall in this season: _____
2. Without question: undou_____ly

80

3. The rat _____ed his way through the bars of the cage. (Rhymes with "board".)
4. A painful complaint affecting the joints:
   r_____matism
5. Six, seven, _____
6. Cars discharge these fumes: ex_____
7. She ate the _____ole cake and left nothing.
8. This man is not _____ to me. (Rhymes with "moan".)
9. Go down: de_____
10. To declare guilty is to cond_____.

The answers are on page 144. If you score 9 out of 10 you may omit this section.

1. Use the words in the box to complete the sentences following.

debt	fasten	writer	rhythm	doubt
hours	know	autumn	psychologist	shepherd

(a) Something you owe is a _____. (d)
(b) _____ means regularity of movement. (R)
(c) To secure or to fix is to _____. (f)
(d) To hesitate or question is to _____. (d)
(e) An author is a _____. (w)
(f) One who deals with the science of human and animal behaviour is a _____. (p)
(g) To be familiar with is to _____. (k)
(h) There are twenty-four _____ in a day. (h)
(i) Spring, summer, _____ and winter are seasons. (a)
(j) A person who tends sheep is a _____. (s)

2. Insert one of the words in the box in each of the sentences following.

Wednesday	descend	subtle	condemn	gnomes
exhausted	would	weigh	ghost	whether

(a) To doom means to _____. (c)
(b) The opposite of ascend is _____. (d)
(c) If you are tired out, you are _____. (e)
(d) _____ means cunning and discerning. (S)
(e) The fourth day of the week is _____. (W)
(f) Young children often believe in _____, fairies and elves. (g)
(g) An apparition or phantom is a _____. (g)
(h) To find the heaviness of something we _____ it. (w)
(i) You must come _____ you like it or not. (Rhymes with "feather".) (w)
(j) If I could I _____. (w)

3. Write the following words and underline the silent letter or letters in each:

brought	debt	rheumatism
descend	fasten	shepherd
rhythm	exhausted	autumn
condemn	whether	ghost
hours	gnome	writer

4. Complete the following sentences with words that have silent letters.
   (a) When you owe money you have a d_____.
   (b) The day following Tuesday is W_____.
   (c) If in d_____ turn back.
   (d) He planned to d_____ the well. (go down)
   (e) In his haste he neglected to f_____ the gate.

5. Disentangle the following letters to make words with a silent letter or letters:
   (a) nnokw (begins with "k")
   (b) hrmhty (begins with "r")
   (c) taesxhu (begins with "e")
   (d) besltu (begins with "s")
   (e) etdb (begins with "d")
   (f) irrtew (begins with "w")

6. Rewrite the following sentences, spelling correctly the words with silent letters.
   (a) It is not nown wether the det will be repaid by Wensday.
   (b) The condemd man was undowtedly guilty.
   (c) The riter worked such long ours that he was exausted.

82

(d) It was a sutle move but I did not dout that it wood succeed.

(e) She was advised to way the advisability or otherwise of consulting a sychiatrist.

We have looked at words with silent consonants; there are also many words with silent vowels. Some words that we spell with "gu" were originally written without the "u". The influence of the French language is responsible for a "u" being written in those words today. Scholars introduced a "u" to "guard" and "guarantee" even though these two words did not have a "u" when written in French.

Here are some "gu" words:

guard	guarantee	guess	guest	guide
guild	guillotine	guilt	guise	guitar

You may remember the "gu" words:

(i)   by recalling the letter order of the words or by "seeing" the words;

(ii) by exaggerating the sounds to yourself, e.g. "goo-ard";

(iii) by associating the words in a silly sentence, e.g.,

"I guess that you will guard the guitar."

Note: "gauge" does not follow the "gu" pattern.

7. Without looking above, write as many "gu" words as you can remember. Check with the list above when you have finished your own list.

8. Write your own silly sentence using "gu" words. Include the word "guard".

"Luncheon" and "surgeon" are often written correctly by people who misspell "pigeon". Association of the three words may help the uncertain speller — luncheon, surgeon, pigeon.

REMINDER

Revision is important.

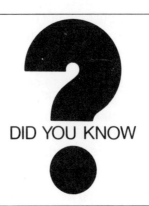

DID YOU KNOW

DICTIONARIES IN ENGLAND

Since the fifteenth century dictionaries of a sort have existed. These early dictionaries merely gave explanations of difficult Latin and other foreign words that were used at the time in England.

In 1582 a headmaster named Mulcaster published a book in which he said that there was a great need for a dictionary showing all English

words. He suggested that the "e" on the end of many words should show that the inside vowel was long (representing the alphabet sound), e.g. "name". Before this time some writers doubled the vowel to show that it was long — "naam" or "naame". We still use some words in which the long vowel sound is shown by doubling the vowel — "keep" is an example.

In eighteenth-century England Samuel Johnson worked for seven years to compile a dictionary. He recorded the spellings of the day, made some alterations — not all of them logical — and wrote in such a pleasing style that the dictionary became a bestseller and was used for a hundred years. People turned to it when they wanted to know how to spell a word and that had the effect of fixing spelling. We still spell most of our words in the same way as Johnson spelt them in his dictionary in 1755.

A dictionary that was published in 1928 was the work of teams of scholars over a period of seventy years. Known as the *New English Dictionary on Historical Principles* it was later re-named the *Oxford English Dictionary*. It gives a complete history of most of the words used since the twelfth century and shows the changes in meaning of each word since that time. This dictionary is so large that it is published in thirteen volumes.

WORDS WITH "PH"

Answers begin page 145

If you see a word with "ph" for the "f" sound you can be fairly confident that the original or root word was Greek. A few words have been simplified and are now spelt with "f" but other words from the same root are still spelt with "ph", e.g., fantasy, phantom.

Test what you know about words with "ph"

Complete the "ph" or "f" words in these sentences.

1. The tel_____ provides a means of speaking to a person at a distance.
2. A pam_____t is a paper-covered booklet.
3. If a thing is unreal or grotesque, it is _____tastic.
4. To talk irreverently about God is to blas_____.
5. A pro_____t foretells the future.
6. A spectre or apparition is a _____tom.
7. A book written by a person about his own life is an auto_____.
8. To deaden or to make stupid is to stup_____y.
9. My cousins are my parents' nieces or n_____.
10. A child bereaved of one or both parents is an or_____.

The answers are on page 145. If you have 9 of the 10 answers correct you may omit this section.

1. Choose words from below to complete the sentences following.

phenomenon   telephone   phantom
pharmacist   physics   physical

(a) The _____ is a useful means of communication.
(b) A person who dispenses drugs is a _____.
(c) An unusual occurrence is a _____.
(d) A spectre or apparition is a _____.
(e) Planned exercise of the body is _____ education.
(f) A science dealing with the laws of nature is _____.

2. From an old Greek word *propheteia* we have two similar words that mean different things: the noun "prophecy" (say prof-e-see), which means "the actual event foretold"; the verb "prophesy" (the "sy" rhymes with "sky"), which means "to foretell the future". Insert the correct word in these sentences.

(a) The _____ of the old chief came true.
(b) I heard her _____ the great storm.
(c) What was the _____ of the wizard?
(Remember: "sy" rhymes with "sky".)

3. Write the correctly spelt words from this list:

fantam   physique   telefone
fantasy   fallacy   pamphlet
profecy   blaspheme   falcon

REMINDER

Do you take a chance or do you check your spelling?

---

4. "Phone" is from a Greek root meaning "sound". Choose from the words below to complete the sentences.

phonograph   microphone
symphony   phrase

(a) To make a small sound louder we use a _____.
(b) A _____ is part of a sentence.
(c) A _____ is music composed for a full orchestra.
(d) A _____ was an early gramophone.

5. "Physics" is from a Greek word meaning "nature". Choose from the words below to complete the sentences.

physics   physical
physique   physician
physiology

(a) The build or bodily structure of a man is his _____.
(b) The science which deals with the laws of nature is

_____.
(c) A medical practitioner is a _____.
(d) If it is to do with the body, it is _____.
(e) The study of living things is _____.

6. Write correct spellings of these "ph" words:

emfatick   telegraff   pamflet
fotograff   fizeek   blasfeem
orfun   fizishun   fobeea

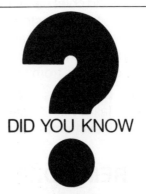

DID YOU KNOW

AN AMERICAN DICTIONARY

In 1783 Noah Webster published a book which became known as *The American Spelling Book*. This book was very popular, but most of the words were spelt as Samuel Johnson had spelt them in his dictionary published twenty-eight years earlier. At the time Webster seemed to be against much change in the spelling system — for example, he stated that "honour" should have a "u" and that it would be more sensible to drop the "o". Do you agree?

After the publication of *The American Spelling Book* Noah Webster became more and more keen to simplify spelling. He suggested, for instance, that "give" should be written "giv" and "laugh" should be "laf". Many, many children would agree that such changes should be made, but Webster seemed to change his mind only gradually.

When he published his book *An American Dictionary of the English Language* in 1828 Webster used "center", "color", "defense" and "favor" instead of the English spellings "centre", "colour", "defence" and "favour". Most of the simplified words in his dictionary were those that distinguish American from English spelling today — words such as "color", "honor" and "traveler". He did not use other simplified words such as "'bred" (bread) that he had recommended twenty-five years earlier.

In England some of Webster's ideas were thought to be worthwhile and Englishmen dropped the "k" from "musick" and "publick". Johnson had attached the "k" to show the Anglo-Saxon origins of the words. Webster's idea of writing "centre" as "center" was not taken up in England, but through advances in transport and printing people on both sides of the Atlantic are now used to such alternatives as center/centre, curb/kerb, favor/favour, gray/grey, jewelry/jewellery, program/programme. It is possible that the simpler spelling will gradually become popular, but, as was pointed out long ago, it is easier to spell "central" from "centre" than from "center". On the other hand, it is more difficult to make a case for keeping the "u" in "colour" and the other "our" words.

89

REVISION VI

Most of the silent letters in words that we use today were once pronounced. The "b" was once pronounced in "dumb" and the "l" was pronounced in "should" and "would". The word "fasten" is from *fast*, but nowadays the "t" is rarely sounded. "Wednesday" is from "Woden's day". (Woden was a Norse god.)

Latin and Greek words are responsible for some of our silent letters: "autumn" from *autumnus*, "column" from *columna*, "condemn" from *condemno*, and "hymn" from *hymnos* (a festive song). We no longer pronounce the endings but we still write the "n" at the end of these words. The "b" has been left in "doubt" because it is from *dubitare* (to be uncertain). "Salmon" is from the Latin *salmo* where the "l" was pronounced. "Rhyme", "rhubarb", "rheumatism" and "rhythm", all beginning with "rh", are words from the Greek. If you have a problem with a particular silent letter, check the origin of the word in a dictionary. The entry for "rhinoceros", for example, may tell you that the word is from two Greek words, *rhino* meaning "the nose" and *keros* meaning "horn" — a horn nose.

Most of the "ph" words we use are from Greek roots. There is no rule to help you know whether to use "ph" or "f". It may help if you can remember the root. For example:

graphein (to write) — autograph, paragraph, biography, graphite

phone (sound) — telephone, phonics, videophone

photo (light) — phosphorus, photograph

physikos (natural) — physique, physical, physiology

Complete the "ie" rule:
    "When the sound is 'ee' write _____."
(Look at page 59 again if you are uncertain.)

90

MINOR TEST VI

1. Complete each of the words below, by adding either "ie" or "ei". (Say the rule to yourself before you start.)

--ghty	fr--ght	p--ce
hyg--ne	y--ld	pr--st
dec--ve	rec--ve	c--ling
w--ght	l--sure	misch--f

2. Write the "ing" form of the following words:

skate	sail
begin	ship
hop	commit
knit	tap
write	rot

3. Complete these sentences. All of the incomplete words have silent letters.
   (a) Scrooge saw three g_____. (spirits)
   (b) After his ordeal he was ex_ _____d. (tired and weak)
   (c) I save for_____n coins. (from another country)
   (d) The aircraft had a great rate of as_____t. (going up)
   (e) The season before winter is a _____.
   (f) I did not borrow money because I dislike being in d_____t. (owing money)

4. Complete the words in these sentences.
   (a) A thin, paper-covered booklet is called a pam_____let.
   (b) We saw the medicine man's pro_____y come true. (telling the future)
   (c) It was an unusual happening. It was a _____enomenon.

5. Add "ous", "eous" or "ious" to each of the words below, making any spelling changes that might be necessary.

   mischief advantage courage grief space

The answers are on page 133. Revise the appropriate section if you have made any errors.

13

CONSONANTS BEFORE "ED"

Answers begin page 146

This section is a development of an earlier section, "Long and short vowel sounds". It deals with an important group of words in which the stress is on the first part of the word when spoken, e.g., we say VISit and not visIT.

It also deals with some words that end with "ic", e.g. "panic". These words take a "k" before "ed" is added.

Test what you know about consonants before "ed"

Complete the words in these sentences by adding "ed" endings and making any spelling changes that are necessary.

1. The passing motorist offer___ to help.
2. "What happen___?" asked the policeman.
3. She visit___ the jail every week.
4. The passengers panic___ as fire swept through the ship.
5. We took sandwiches and coffee and picnic___ on the beach.
6. Poor families benefit___ from the money contributed.
7. The convict had commit___ only minor crimes.

8. She butter___ the bread.
9. I prefer___ the early part of the concert.
10. Swimming is not permit___ here.

The answers are on page 146. If you have more than one spelling wrong you should work through this section.

We often need to add "ed" or "ing" to a word of more than one syllable. The way we say the word usually indicates whether the last letter of the word is doubled or not. If the stress is on the last syllable the last consonant is doubled.

Say the word "happen" and notice where you stress it. The stress is on the first syllable, so we do not double the "n" when adding a suffix to make "*happ*ened".

Now say "begin". The stress is on the second syllable, "gin", so we double the "n" to make "be*ginn*ing".

We strengthen the end by doubling the consonant if the stress is near the end, e.g., re*fer* (stress is at the end) — referred.

1. (a) Say the words below. Consider where each word is stressed. Decide whether you would double the final consonant before adding a suffix.

benefit	equip	differ
order	admit	refer
permit	offer	open
occur	visit	omit

(b) Write each word and add "ed".

93

Note: "Reference" has one "r", the stress being on the first syllable, but in "referral" the "r" is doubled.

Words ending with "ic" take a "k" before a suffix, e.g., panic — panicked, picnic — picnicking. Can you see why the "k" is necessary?

2. Add the suffix "ed" to the words in the box and then complete the sentences below. Note: "traffic" is a special case. See page 93.

> visit   offer   regret   benefit
> traffic   permit   refer   happen

(a) A millionaire offer___ to purchase the painting.
(b) The manager regret___ the delay.
(c) The children visit___ the museum.
(d) Police asked witnesses how the accident happen___.
(e) Parking on the grass is not permit___.
(f) The duke benefit___ from the will.
(g) "You have traffic___ in drugs," said the judge.
(h) The principal refer___ to the student's past record.

3. The purpose of this exercise is to help you check that you recognise the stressed syllables in words.

(a) Write these words. Say them. Underline the part you stress.

> begin   commit   benefit   toboggan
> gallop   refer   occur   prefer

(b) Now add "ing" endings to the words. You must decide whether the last consonant should be doubled.

REMINDER

Double the last consonant if the last syllable is stressed.

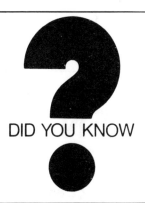

DID YOU KNOW

ETYMOLOGY IN THE DICTIONARY

A good dictionary gives a brief history of words, which often helps to explain rather odd spellings.

who (hōō), *pron.* any person, that person, what person? (O.E. hwa).

(O.E. hwa: "who" was an Old English word spelt "hwa".)

As the Saxons spelt the word "hwa" they must have pronounced it that way. That explains why we still spell the word with a "w".

Use your dictionary to find the original spellings (and pronunciations) of these words: white, where, whisper, whistle, whole, whine, while, whether, when, wheel, wharf, whale.

Sometimes a word can be traced through more than one language.

degree (di-grē′), *n.* relative position, rank or grade, geographical measurement, an award of a university or college. (Fr. degré f. *LL degradus*).

(The last few words in the above entry show that the word "degree" comes from the French word *degré* but that the French word is from a Latin word *degradus*.)

Sometimes we use two old words to make a modern word.

telephone (tel′ĕ-fōn), *n.* electrical instrument for transmitting spoken conversation over a distance. (Gk *tele* — far, *phone* — sound).

(The last few words in this entry show that the word "telephone" comes from two Greek words meaning "far" and "sound".)

95

14

WORD ENDINGS — "CEDE", "CEED" AND "SEDE"

Answers begin page 147

Each of these word endings is pronounced "seed". "Cede" is the most commonly used ending; there are four exceptions. The following pages will help you to remember the exceptions.

Test what you know about these word endings

Add the "cede", "ceed" or "sede" ending to each of the incomplete words in the following sentences.

1. If at first you do not suc_____ you should try, try and try again.
2. This is the new model which will super_____ that one.
3. Let the search pro_____.
4. To admit that something is true is to con_____.
5. To pass the limit is to ex_____ the limit.
6. If I speak on someone's behalf I inter_____ for him.
7. To go before is to pre_____.
8. To go back is to re_____.

The answers are on page 147. If you have 7 out of 8 correct you may omit this section.

In most words that end with the "seed" sound, the last syllable is spelt "cede". Remember these exceptions and you should have no problems:

supersede — the only word with the "sede" ending;

proceed ⎫
succeed ⎬ — the only three words with the "ceed" ending.
exceed ⎭

All other similar-sounding words end with "cede".

REMINDER

Super- takes "s" (supersede), and pro-, suc-, ex- are the only three to take "ceed".

1. Complete the following rule:

   Super- takes "s" and pro-, suc-, ex- are the only three to take

   _____.

2. Add the correct endings to these words. Do not hesitate to refer to the rule above.

   (a) inter_____   (d) super_____   (g) re_____
   (b) con_____   (e) pre_____   (h) ex_____
   (c) pro_____   (f) suc_____   (i) ac_____

3 (a) Which word ends with "sede"?
   (b) Which three words end with "ceed"?
   (c) What ending does con_____ have?
   (d) Complete the rule: _____ takes "s."
   (e) Complete the rule: "Pro-, suc-, ex- take _____."

4. Write the correct word from each group below. Two spellings in each line are incorrect.

   (a) superceed   supercede   supersede
   (b) proceed   procede   prosede
   (c) exceed   excede   exsede
   (d) succeed   succede   sucsede

5. Complete each of the sentences below with an appropriate word from the box.

intercede	recede
proceed	accede
supersede	succeed

(a) You will suc____ if you keep trying.
(b) When something goes back it is said to re____.
(c) To go on is to pro____.
(d) To replace something is to super____ it.
(e) When someone settles a quarrel that person is said to inter____.
(f) To agree to someone's request is to ac____ to his wishes.

6. Complete the following:
(a) To plead in favour of a person is to inter____.
(b) Pro-, suc- and ex- take ____.
(c) Motorists may be fined if they ex____ the speed limit.
(d) To surrender or give in is to con____.
(e) Super- takes ____.
(f) Most words in this section take ____.
(g) When I go on I pro____.
(h) If I obey someone I ac____ to his request.

REMINDER

Have you made a short-list of your own spelling demons?

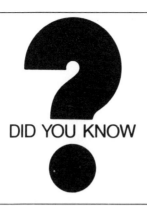

DID YOU KNOW

AND STILL MORE ODDITIES

The Saxons who lived in England a thousand years ago said "hwaer", "hwit" and "hwaete"; today we say "where", "white" and "wheat". If you are from Scotland you may sound the "h", but in England three or four hundred years ago the "w" was placed first in the spellings of the words because the "h" was no longer sounded.

Most of our "wh" words were originally "hw" words. Here are some original words and the modern ones that have replaced them:

hwy——▶ why	hweol——▶ wheel	hwistlian——▶ whistle
hwat——▶ what	hwil——▶ while	hwisprian——▶ whisper
hwaenne——▶ when	hwearf——▶ wharf	hwinan——▶ whinny

In the words "who" (O.E. hwa) and "whom" (O.E. hwam) it is the "h" that is now pronounced and the "w" that is silent. The spellings of those words were changed so that they fitted the pattern of the other "wh" words.

The letters "ee" and "ea" once represented different sounds. Pronunciation changed and although both pairs of letters now represent the "ee" sound in many words, we still use both "ee" and "ea" in our spellings. Some words that were borrowed from the French were spelt with "ie" to represent an "ee" sound and, rather carelessly, a few Old English words were also spelt with "ie".

Unfortunately, not all words that we spell with "ea" changed their pronunciations to an "ee" sound and so we have words with varied pronunciations such as "pleasant", "death", "earth" and "bear".

REVISION VII

Word endings — "ed" and "ing"
Do you double the last letter of "gallop" or "occur" before adding a suffix such as "ed" or "ing"?

Rule: Say the word. If the stress is on the last sound you double the last letter.

For example:
  (a) In *"gallop"* the stress is on the first syllable. We do not double the last letter — "galloping".
  (b) In *"occur"* the stress is on the second syllable. We double the last letter — "occurred".

If the last letter is an "l", it is always doubled when a suffix is added, as in quarrel — quarrelled, cancel — cancelled.

Word endings — "sede", "cede", "ceed"
Remember, super- takes "s" (supersede).
Pro-, suc-, ex- are the only three to take "ceed" (proceed, succeed, exceed).

Plurals
Plurals of words that end with an "f" change the "f" to "ves" when becoming plural, as in half — halves, knife — knives, thief — thieves.

  Exceptions are "oo" words, such as roof — roofs, hoof — hoofs (hooves is acceptable), proof — proofs.

  Words that end with "o" take "es" when they become plural, for example, potato — potatoes, mosquito — mosquitoes. Most musical words do not follow this rule.

MINOR TEST VII

1. Say the following words and notice where they are stressed. Write the words and add "ed" endings.

visit		commit
	transfer	
offer		permit

2. Add "ceed", "sede" or "cede" to complete each of the following words:

pro_____   suc_____   inter_____   ex_____
super_____   con_____   ac_____   re_____

3. How would you make plurals of words that end with "y"
   (a) when there is a vowel before the "y", as in "monkey"?
   (b) when there is a consonant before the "y", as in "country"?

4. Write the plurals of
   (a) life   shelf   wolf   loaf   roof   thief
   (b) tomato   echo   zoo   solo   piano

5. Complete the following sentences by choosing the correct word from those in brackets.
   (a) I am not sure _____ to take a raincoat. (whether, weather)
   (b) It is nearly half _____ ten. (past, passed)
   (c) That man was _____ an athlete. (formally, formerly)
   (d) I bought pens and _____. (stationary, stationery)
   (e) Please put it down _____. (there, their)

Turn to page 134 for the answers. Revise the appropriate section if you have made any errors.

15

WORD ENDINGS — "ABLE" AND "IBLE"

Answers begin page 148

There is no clear rule to distinguish words that end with "able" from those that end with "ible".

Test what you know about these word endings

Complete the words in these sentences with "a" or "i".

1. If a person is obstinate and unbending he is inflex–ble.
2. Such cold weather is unseason–ble at this time of year.
3. If something is unbelievable or too improbable to accept we say it is incred–ble.
4. Butter and bacon are both perish–ble foods.
5. A disease that cannot be cured is incur–ble.
6. The committee's decision was debat–ble.
7. It was permiss–ble for the students to answer only three questions on the exam paper.
8. If something is fit to eat it is ed–ble.
9. A wide choice of goods was avail–ble in the shops.
10. Something that can be divided is said to be divis–ble.

The answers are on page 148. If you have 9 out of 10 correct you may omit this section.

If the root word is written in full the most usual ending is "able", as in notice — noticeable (the "e" keeps the "c" soft), credit — creditable.

It is best to learn the troublesome words by sound. Do not bother about the words that you know.

Step A: If the root word is used the suffix is likely to be "able".

Step B: Learn the words that you are likely to use by exaggerating the end sound.

Step C: Be sure to write incorrectly spelt words in your *Word Book* and **revise**!

Do you add "able" or "ible" to "drink"? As the whole word will be used, the probable ending is "able". Check the above list. Remember the end by stressing the sound to yourself — drink*able*.

1. Try these words. Refer to Steps A and B above to decide whether to add "able" or "ible".
   (a) respect
   (b) remark
   (c) notice (the "e" keeps the "c" soft)
   (d) horr- (only part of the word)
   (e) suit
   (f) profit
   (g) favour

2. Decide whether you would use "able" or "ible" for each of the words or parts of words below. Use the method described earlier to help you decide.

terr-	manage (keep the "e")
work	aud-
enjoy	fashion
poss-	plaus-

3. Try these, again using the method described:

agree	work	peace (keep the "e")
incred-	permiss-	pronounce (keep the "e")
perish	divis-	uncontrol(l)

Important: The method described above does not work with the following words. They end with "able" even though the base word is not complete. Say the words. Stress the "able".

charit-	hospit-	inevit-
dur-	formid-	navig-
irrit-	vulner-	impecc-

Add "able" to these words or parts of words and pronounce them carefully. Say "able" clearly.

negoti-	unmistak-	mov-
credit	recognis-	respect
desir-	perish	sale
objection	li-	service
ador-	advis-	inflamm-

REMINDER

Get a clear sound recording of "able" words in your mind.

If you have difficulty in remembering a particular "able" word, try the word-association method. It works like this: When you have difficulty with "profitable", but you know "agreeable", simply remember

"It is profitable to be agreeable"

or invent your own silly sentence using "able" words. For example:

"It was unmistakable that the dog was manageable and teachable."

A few complete words take the ending "ible". For example:

contemptible   convertible   resistible   repressible

Some "able" words:

adorable	honourable	peaceable
advisable	impracticable	perishable
agreeable	incurable	pleasurable
available	inevitable	profitable
believable	justifiable	recognisable
changeable	likeable	reliable
charitable	lovable	removable
considerable	manageable	respectable
debatable	miserable	serviceable
durable	movable	sociable
excitable	notable	teachable
fashionable	payable	unmistakable

Note: "S" or "z" may be used in "recognisable".

105

Some "ible" words:

audible	forcible	permissible
credible	incredible	plausible
divisible	indestructible	responsible
edible	indigestible	reversible
eligible	irresistible	sensible
feasible	legible	tangible
flexible	negligible	visible

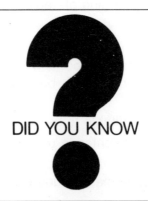

DID YOU KNOW

ASSIMILATION

We often use two English words as one, e.g., "bookcase", "schoolgirl". We call those words "compound words".

Many of the words we use today are derived from Latin words with Latin prefixes such as *ad* meaning "to" or "toward". It is often awkward to say "ad" in front of a word. For example, it is not as easy to say "adrive" as "arrive", and it is easier to say "accept" than "adcept".

Here are some variations of *ad*:

ac — according	ad — admire	af — affect
ag — aggressive	al — ally	an — announce
ap — applaud	ar — arrogant	as — assemble
	at — attend	

Changing the "d" to make it the same as the first letter of the root is called "assimilation".

The prefix "in" means "not" or "against", or sometimes "into". Here are some examples of assimilation:

im-migrate   il-legal   ir-regular

Try to say the word "disfer". If you find it easier to say "differ" you will understand why the "dis" changed to "dif".

The same sort of thing happened to some English words and they now sound more pleasant. The Old English word "wifman" became "wimman" and the spelling later changed to "woman".

English has become a less harsh language than it once was. We still have some words that do not roll off the tongue; for example, "eighths", "wasps" and "tempts" are a little clumsy. On the other hand, we have lost the "gh" sound in words such as "might", the "k" in "knight" and the "g" in "gnaw", the "l" in "should" and "would", and the "b" in "dumb" and "comb".

PREFIXES — TO DOUBLE OR NOT?

Answers begin page 148

Dissatisfied, disappoint — are you sure that these two spellings are correct?

Test what you know about prefixes

Complete the following sentences by adding the correct prefix to each of the words in italic (slanting) type. In most cases, adding the prefix will give you the opposite of the word in italics.

1. I have often seen that naughty child __*behave*.
2. Did the conjurer make the rabbit __*appear*?
3. "Enjin" is a __*spelling* of "engine".
4. The car is clean so it is __*necessary* to wash it.
5. Please help me to __*tangle* the wool.
6. The number of __*migrants* to the country has risen. (people settling here)
7. He __*calculated* the angle of the shot.
8. Thoughts of his __*spent* youth returned.
9. The committee's decision will be __*reversible*, so they will think carefully before changing the rules.
10. Return the goods if you are __*satisfied*.

The answers are on page 148. If you have more than one wrong, you should work through this section.

The prefix "mis" means "bad" or "badly"; for example, "to misbehave" means "to behave badly".

1 (a) What do the following words mean when the prefix "mis" is added?

judge   conduct   calculate
adventure   behave   manage

(b) Add "mis" to this word and write it in full:

spell

How many times did you write the letter "s"? Can you see why?

(c) Put "mis" before the following words:

spent   shaped   print

What do you notice about the first two new words? What do the new words mean?

The prefix "dis" means "not"; for example, "to disbelieve" means "to not believe".

2 (a) What do the following words mean when "dis" is added?

appoint   appear

How many times did you write the letter "s"? Why?

(b) Now add "dis" to the following words:

satisfied   service   similar

What does each new word mean? Can you see why each of the three words has a double "s" where the prefix joins the base word?

The prefix "un" can mean "not". It can also mean the opposite of an action, as in "undress". For example:

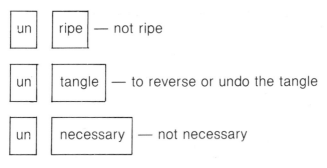

| un | ripe | — not ripe |

| un | tangle | — to reverse or undo the tangle |

| un | necessary | — not necessary |

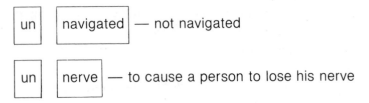

un | navigated | — not navigated

un | nerve | — to cause a person to lose his nerve

3 (a) Write the word that means "not natural"?
  (b) How many times did you write "n"?
  (c) Why?

By adding the prefix "im" to root words we can decide how to spell many of the "im" words; "im" means "not" or "in".

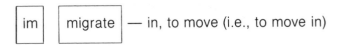

im | migrate | — in, to move (i.e., to move in)

4. Write the words that mean:
  (a) not possible
  (b) not personal
  (c) not mature
  (d) to put in prison
  (e) not plausible
  (f) not moral
  (g) too great to be measured (*Mensura* is Latin for "measure".)

The prefix "ir" also means "not". Decide how many "r's" there are in the word meaning "not relevant".
5. Write the words that mean not recoverable, not rational, not responsible, not reversible, not regular.
Notice what happens when "ir" is added to a word beginning with "r".
Note the spelling of "irreparable" (not able to be repaired).

REVISION VIII

The suffixes "able" and "ible"
Add "able" to words that are already complete, and "ible" to most incomplete words. For example: "fashion" is a complete word. It is likely to take "able" — "fashionable". "Incred" is not a complete word. You will probably not add "able" — "incredible".

An "e" is kept at the end of a base word (or root) to keep a "c" or "g" soft. See page 104 for an exception. Try to remember the sounds of the words.

Prefixes

Think of the prefix and base word as being separate. For example:

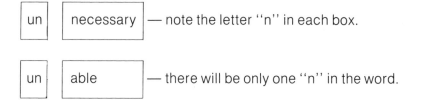

Spelling rule
When the sound is "ee" write "i" before "e" except after "c". For example:

    ch__f   — this word makes an "ee" sound. Follow the rule and write "ie".

    dec__ve — this word makes an "ee" sound, but the two letters are after "c". Write "ei".

    h__ght   — this word does not make an "ee" sound so do not follow the rule — write "ei".

Write the complete words.

111

Word endings

To keep a vowel short when you add "ing" or "ed" you should double the last consonant. The vowel is usually long if you leave only one consonant at the end of the base word. For example:

write, writing — the long sound is kept.

write, written — the double consonant makes the first vowel short.

MINOR TEST VIII

1. Write the three-step method of remembering whether a word is likely to have an "able" or "ible" suffix.

2 (a) Write the plurals of the words below and sort them into two groups:

Group 1 — words to which you simply add "s" to make plurals,

Group 2 — words in which the "y" is dropped and "ies" is added.

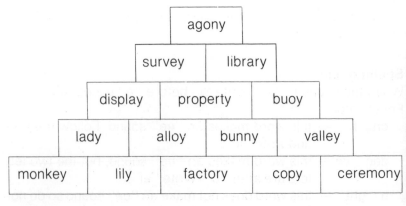

(b) What do you notice about the letters before "y" in Group 1?

3. The answers to the clues below are words that contain silent letters. Write the words in full.
   (a) A weekday (W)
   (b) Elves, _____ and pixies (g)
   (c) Sung in church (h)
   (d) One of the seasons (a)
   (e) Something one must repay (d)
   (f) Car's fumes (ex)

4 (a) Write the word that ends with "sede".
   (b) Write three words that end with "ceed".

5. Write each word in full by inserting either "ie" or "ei".
   (a) th--f   (c) p--ce
   (b) w--gh   (d) rec--ve

6. Add "ed", "en" or "ing" to the words below. You must decide what to do about the last letter of each word.

write	slip	pull	entice
bit	hope	race	wrap

7. Write the "ie" rule.

Turn to page 134 for the answers. Revise the appropriate section if you have made any errors.

MAJOR SPELLING TEST

Insert the missing letters to complete the words in these sentences.

1. Two quarters make a half. Two h_____s make a whole.
2. It was a courag_____s act.
3. Please collect three l_____s of bread.
4. Will you write their names and ad_____s please?
5. The flies and mosq_____s were troublesome.
6. The elf gave a misch____v____s grin.
7. A small paper-covered booklet is a pam_____.
8. We visi_____d the island once more.
9. Our boat hap_____d to be passing.
10. We picnic_____ on the beach.
11. I off_____d to remain behind.
12. Her story dif_____d from his account.
13. The cup was accid_____y broken.
14. He read the paper critic_____y.
15. "Yours since_____y" is sometimes written at the end of a letter.
16. The tea was made aut_____ly by the machine.
17. The Indian ch_____f slowly folded his arms.
18. My nephew and my n_____ce called today.
19. What is the h_____t of that building?
20. You must forf_____t the goods you tried to smuggle.
21. Rates and tax_____ must be paid.
22. The guide replied to many enq_____.
23. "Innocent until proven g_____y" is a basic principle of our legal system.
24. Proof of payment is shown by a rec_____t.
25. After the long run he was ex_____d.
26. Keep trying and you will suc_____.

114

27. Please do not ex_____ the speed limit.
28. The player was transf_____d to another club.
29. The brothers quarrel_____d over the money.
30. The whole school ben_____d from the generous gift.

When you have finished the test turn to page 131 for the answers. Ask someone to check your work in case you have missed any errors. Enter any words you had wrong in your *Word Book*. Graph your result on page 150.

APPENDIX

Mnemonics

A mnemonic is an aid to the memory.

Bachelor: the bachelor has no "t".

Business: take a *bus in* to your business.

Cemetery: "e's" are the only vowels buried in the cemetery.

Privilege: "leg" as in "legal". (Privilege comes from a Latin word meaning "private law".)

All right: two words like "all wrong".

Supersede: begins with "s" and is the only common word to end with "sede" (with an "s").

Grammar: take off the "g" and then it is spelt the same way forwards and backwards.

Parallel: the middle two "l's" are parallel.

Piece: have a *piece* of *pie*.

Believe: see the *lie* in be*lie*ve.

Hear: you h*ear* with your *ear*.

Here
There }: w*here*? *here* and t*here*.
Where

See the section on homonyms for more mnemonic devices.

Some common Latin roots

Root	Root meaning	Some English words from the root
annus	a year	annual, anniversary, biennial
aqua	water	aquarium, aquatic, aqueduct
audio	hear	audible, audience, audition

116

bene	well, good	benefit, benefactor, benevolence
cado	fall	accident, incident, case
capio	take	captive, capable, accept
caput	the head	capital, captain, cattle
cedo	go	accede, exceed, proceed
claudo	close	include, conclude
credo	believe	creed, credible, credit
dico	say	dictionary, dictate, contradict
duco	lead	reduce, produce, educate
facio	make	factory, fact, factor
fero	carry	refer, suffer, transfer
frango	break	fraction, fracture, infringe
fluo	flow	fluid, fluent, affluent
fundo	pour	foundry, refund, fuse
gradior	step	gradual, grade, graduate
gratus	thankful	grateful, gratuity
jacio	throw	eject, conjecture, inject
judex	judge	judge, judgement, prejudice
manus	hand	manufacture, manner, manage
magnus	great	magnify, magnificent
migro	migrate	migrate, immigrant, emigrant
miles	soldier	military, militant
mitto	send	missile, mission, admit
mors	death	mortal, mortgage, post-mortem
porto	carry	porter, report, import
primus	first	primary, primitive, prince
scribo	write	script, scribble, describe
spiro	breathe	expire, conspire, inspire

Some common Greek roots

Root	Root meaning	Some English words from the root
astron	star	asterisk, astrology, astronaut, astronomy
derma	the skin	dermatitis, dermatologist, hypodermic
graphein	to write	autograph, graph, graphic, graphite, paragraph, telegraph

hugies	healthy	hygiene
hudor	water	dehydrate, hydrant, hydraulic, hydrogen, hydroplane
kuklos	a circle	bicycle, cyclone
logos	a word	astrology, catalogue, dialogue, epilogue, logic, monologue, prologue
metros	to measure	meter, metric, thermometer, speedometer
mikros	small	microbe, micrometer, microfilm, microphone, microscope
monos	alone, one	monoplane, monologue, monopoly, monotone
pathos	feeling	antipathy, pathetic, sympathy
phone	sound	microphone, phonic, telephone
plassein	to mould	plastic, plaster
platus	broad, level	plate, platitude, plateau
polis	a city	metropolitan, police, policy, politics
photo	a light	photocopy, photograph
skopeo	see	microscope, periscope, telescope

Some spelling demons

Have four dictated to you daily.

academic
accessible
accommodation
1. address ✓
affect (verb)
2. alcohol ✓
3. all right ✓ 4. alright
amateur
among
analyse
annual ✓
5. arguing ✓
athlete
auxiliary
6. awful ✓

awkward
balance
balloon
7. beginning ✓
believe ✓
benefited
breathe (verb)
buried
business
calculator ⑨
camouflage ✗
carburettor
catastrophe
changeable ⑧
coconut

118

committee (10)
comparative
conscience (11)
control
courteous
criticism
cylinder
dependant (noun)
dependent (adjective)
despair
desperate (12)
develop
diesel
dietary
dilemma
dinghy (boat)
dispatch
dissatisfied
drunkenness
effect (noun)
efficiency
eighth
eligible
embarrass (13)
emigrant (leaves a country)
environment
exercise
exhilarate
existence
fascinate (14)
February
forecast
fullness
gardener
gauge
grievous
guard
guide
harass
hiccup

humorous (15)
hypocrisy
imaginary
immediately
immigrant (enters a country)
initialled
installation
interpret
interrupt (16)
irresistible
irritable
jackeroo
jealous (17)
jewellery
judgement
kerosene
knowledge (18)
labelled
leisure
liaison
library
lightening (reducing weight)
lightning (flash)
liqueur (Drambuie, for example)
liquor (alcoholic drink)
literature
loneliness (19)
lying
maintenance
manoeuvre (20)
medieval
meteorology
methylated
miniature
mischievous
misdemeanour
misspelt
monastery
mortgage
mysterious

119

necessarily

neighbour

occasion

occurred

official

omission

omit

operate

orthopaedic

pantomime

paraffin

parallel

paralyse

particularly

peaceable

perceive

perseverance

personal (private)

personnel (staff)

perspiration

pneumonia

possess

principal (main)

principle (rule)

pronunciation

psychology

quarrelling

queue

quiet

racket (noise)

racquet (used in tennis)

receipt

receive

recommend

reconnaissance

relevant

relieve

religious

rhythm

ridiculous

rigorous

satellite

scarcely

schedule

seize

separate

sergeant

sincerely

speech

stationary (standing still)

stationery (paper)

strength

succeed

success

surely

surprise

taxis

technique

temperature

temporarily

thorough

tomatoes

transferred

truly

twelfth

until

vacuum

vengeance

verandah

villain

vitamin

Wednesday

weird

whether

wholly

wield

writing

written

Word list

Here is a list of words that occur in this book. The number (or numbers) next to each word will indicate the section (or sections) in which the word occurs.

A

abstemious	9	April	2
academically	7	aquarium	1
accede	14	arches	3
access	6	assassin	6
accidentally	7	athlete	2
accommodation	6	athletics	2
accomplish	6	attend	2
accost	6	attract	1
accouchement	6	audible	15
account	6	autograph	1
accuse	6	automatically	7
addresses	3, 4	autumn	11
admitted	13	awful	2
adorable	15	**B**	
advantageous	9	balance	2
adventurous	9	banjos	4
advice	5	banner	2
advisable	15	basically	7
advise	5	baton	2
affect	2	beauteous	9
agree	15	beginning	2, 6, 13
agreeable	15	belief	8
alien	8	believe	8
all together	5	benediction	1
also	2	benefactor	1
altar	5	benefit	1, 2, 13
alter	5	benefited	13
altogether	5	benefiting	13
altos	4	benevolent	1
amend	2	berries	3, 5
apologetically	7	berry	3, 5
appear	6	betting	10
appoint	2, 6	biography	1

bison	2	climb	10
biting	10	clip	2
blaspheme	12	coarse	5
blessing	2	coated	10
blissful	2	coconut	2
bosun	2	cola	2
bounteous	9	college	2
boxes	3	columns	3
brief	8	commerce	2
brought	11	commission	6
bungalows	3	commit	13
bury	5	committed	13
buses	3	committing	13
button	2	complement	5
C		compliment	5
calendar	2	concede	14
calling	2	conceit	8
calves	4	conceivable	8
candid	2	conceive	8
caning	10	concentrate	2
canning	10	condemn	11
cantos	4	condemned	11
cap	10	conduct	2
cape	10	conscious	9
cargoes	4	contain	1
cashier	8	contemptible	15
cattle	1	contraltos	4
ceiling	8	convertible	15
certainly	7	copies	3
charitable	15	counties	3
chatter	2	countries	3
check	10	courageous	9
cherries	3	course	5
cherry	5	coyly	7
chief	8	crazily	7
child	2	creamed	10
chimneys	3	creditable	15
chin	10	critically	7
claiming	10	cropped	10
classic	2	cruelly	7

foreign	8	guarantee	11
forfeit	8	guard	11
formally	5	guerilla	5
formerly	5	guess	11
formidable	15	guest	11
freight	8	guide	11
frequent	2	guild	11
fundamentally	7	guillotine	11
funnily	7	guilt	11
furious	9	guise	11
fuse	10	guitar	11
fussing	2	**H**	
fuzzy	2	halves	4
		handful	6
G		handkerchief	8
gallop	13	handkerchiefs	4
galloping	13	handkerchieves	4
gaped	10	happened	13
gaping	10	happily	7
gauge	11	harass	2, 6
ghost	11	heifer	8
glorious	9	height	8
gnawed	11	helpful	6
gnomes	11	here	5
gorgeous	9	heroes	4
gorilla	5	hitting	2
gossip	2	holy	2
government	2	hoofs	4
gracious	9	hooves	4
grape	2	hope	10
graph	1	hoped	10
grated	10	hopeful	6
grateful	1	hoping	10
gratify	1	hopping	2, 10
grating	10	horrible	15
gratitude	1	horrid	2
gratuity	1	hospitable	15
grief	8	hours	11
grievance	8	humble	2
grievous	9	humorous	9

125

phobia	12	primeval	1
phone	2, 12	primitive	1
phonograph	12	principal	5
photograph	12	principle	5
photos	4	print	2
phrase	12	privilege	2
physical	12	probably	7
physician	12	proceed	2, 14
physics	12	profitable	15
physiology	12	pronounceable	15
physique	12	proofs	4
pianos	4	properties	3
piccolos	4	prophecy	12
picnicked	13	prophesy	12
piece	8	protract	1
pigeon	11	psychiatrist	11
pilot	2	psychologist	11
pining	10	publicly	7
pinning	10	pulleys	3
pirate	2	punctuation	2
pitches	3	**Q**	
piteous	9	quarrel	6
planing	10	quiet	2
platitude	2		
plausible	15	**R**	
plenteous	9	radio	2
poker	2	radios	4
popular	2	rammed	10
possible	15	rarely	7
potatoes	4	rat	10
practice	5	rate	10
practise	5	recede	14
precede	14	receipt	8
preferred	13	receive	8
prejudice	2	recognisable	15
premier	1	refer	13
previous	9	reference	13
primary	1	referral	13
primate	1	referred	13
prime	1	referring	13

regretted	13	saleable	15
reign	8	sandwich	2
reliably	7	scarfs	4
relief	8	scarves	4
reliefs	4	scrub	10
relieve	8	seated	10
religious	9	secret	2, 10
remark	2	secretary	2
remarkable	15	seize	8
removable	15	selves	4
replies	3	sensibly	7
repressible	15	separate	2
resistible	15	serious	9
respectable	15	serviceable	15
restaurant	2	severely	7
retain	1	shelves	4
retrieve	8	shepherd	11
rheumatism	11	shriek	8
rhythm	11	shyly	7
ridiculous	9	siege	8
rigorous	9	silent	2
riotous	9	Simon	2
ripe	10	simply	7
ripping	10	sincerely	7
rivet	2	sitting	2
robber	2	skilful	6
robbing	2, 10	slapping	10
robe	10	slid	10
robing	10	slide	10
robot	2	sliding	10
roofs	4	slipped	10
rope	10	slyly	7
rotation	2	smallest	2
rotten	2	sober	2
rubbed	10	soccer	2
ruler	2	societies	3
rushing	2	solos	4
S		sopranos	4
safes	4	spacious	9
sagging	10	spinning	10

Answers to major spelling test

1. halves
2. courageous
3. loaves
4. addresses
5. mosquitoes
6. mischievous
7. pamphlet
8. visited
9. happened
10. picnicked
11. offered
12. differed
13. accidentally
14. critically
15. sincerely
16. automatically
17. chief
18. niece
19. height
20. forfeit
21. taxes
22. enquiries
23. guilty
24. receipt
25. exhausted
26. succeed
27. exceed
28. transferred
29. quarrelled
30. benefited

Answers to minor tests

Minor test I (page 21)
1 (a) inspire, expire
   (b) manufacture
   (c) creed, credit
   (d) annual, anniversary
   (e) audience, audition
   (f) telescope
2. possible, usual, prison, guide
3. mis/chie/vous   priv/i/lege   re/com/mend   lin/guis/tic
   in/ter/fere   um/brel/la   to/bac/co   en/dea/vour
   suc/ces/sion   sep/a/rate   qua/ran/tine   cel/e/brate
4. ac/ces/so/ry   ne/ces/sa/ry   ac/com/mo/date   a/mal/ga/mate
   af/fil/i/ate   al/le/vi/ate   oc/ca/sion/al   neu/tra/li/ty
5. hydrant: *hudor* (water). Greek
   magnify: *magnus* (great), *facere* (to make). Latin
   include: *includere* (to shut in). Latin
   photograph: *photos* (light), *graph* (to write). Greek
   fluid: *fluidus* (flowing). Latin
   conclude: *concludere* (to end). Latin

Minor test II (page 36)

1. thieves, potatoes, pianos, mosquitoes, leaves, calves, tomatoes, roofs
2. tragedies, buses, properties, delays, universities, studies

Minor test III (page 51)

1. (a) practice, advice, prophecy
   (b) The nouns are spelt with a "c".
2. (a) passed
   (b) stationary
   (c) their
   (d) coarse
   (e) alter
3. (a) The books on the shelves helped with her studies of monkeys.
   (b) Thank you for your enquiries about the properties we have for sale.
4. (a) classes
   (b) monkeys
   (c) buses
   (d) tragedies
   (e) copies
   (f) journeys

Minor test IV (page 65)

1. (a) stationary
   (b) principal
   (c) lose
   (d) past
   (e) coarse
   (f) there
   (g) its (no apostrophe)
2. (a) proudly
   (b) critically
   (c) fiercely
   (d) apologetically
   (e) probably

(f) drastically
(g) automatically
(h) accidentally
3. If a word ends with "ic" we add "ally". (A notable exception is "publicly".)
4 (a) Simply add "s", e.g., key — keys; monkey — monkeys.
  (b) Change the "y" to "i" and add "es", e.g., lady — ladies.

Minor test V (page 78)

1 (a) receive
  (b) believe
  (c) thieves
  (d) siege
  (e) weigh

2 (a) wheeled   (d) nailing   (g) drummed
  (b) written   (e) shopped   (h) wiping
  (c) placing   (f) skinning   (i) beginning

3 (a) obvious   (e) courageous   (i) humorous
  (b) serious   (f) conscious   (j) delicious
  (c) mischievous   (g) ridiculous   (k) religious
  (d) gracious   (h) mysterious   (l) spacious

Minor test VI (page 91)

1. eighty   freight   piece
  hygiene   yield   priest
  deceive   receive   ceiling
  weight   leisure   mischief

2. skating   sailing
  beginning   shipping
  hopping   committing
  knitting   tapping
  writing   rotting

3 (a) ghosts   (d) ascent
  (b) exhausted   (e) autumn
  (c) foreign   (f) debt

4 (a) pamphlet
  (b) prophecy
  (c) phenomenon

5. mischievous, advantageous, courageous, grievous, spacious

Minor test VII (page 102)

1. visited, committed, transferred, offered, permitted
2. proceed   succeed   intercede   exceed
   supersede   concede   accede   recede
3 (a) Simply add "s".
  (b) Replace the "y" by "ies".
4 (a) lives, shelves, wolves, loaves, roofs, thieves
  (b) tomatoes, echoes, zoos, solos, pianos
5 (a) whether
  (b) past
  (c) formerly
  (d) stationery
  (e) there

Minor test VIII (page 112)

1. Step A: If the suffix is added to a root word, it is likely to be "able".
   Step B: Learn the words by exaggerating the sounds.
   Step C: In your *Word Book*, write any words you misspelt.
2 (a) *Group 1*   *Group 2*
       surveys   agonies   factories
       displays   libraries   copies
       buoys   properties   ceremonies
       alloys   ladies
       valleys   bunnies
       monkeys   lilies
  (b) There is a vowel before the "y" in each word in Group 1.
3 (a) Wednesday   (d) autumn
  (b) gnomes   (e) debt
  (c) hymns   (f) exhaust
4 (a) supersede (Remember that "super" takes "s".)
  (b) proceed, succeed, exceed
5 (a) thief   (b) weigh   (c) piece   (d) receive
6. written or writing   pulled or pulling
   bitten or biting   raced or racing
   slipped or slipping   enticed or enticing
   hoped or hoping   wrapped or wrapping
7. When the sound is "ee" write "i" before "e" except after "c".

Answers to exercises

1 Roots (page 5)
1. Take away
2. To draw out
3. Draws (or pulls) things.
4. Draws (or pulls) things.
5. Octopus, October, octagon, octogenarians, octave, octet. *Octo* means "eight".
6 (a) retain
  (b) contain
  (c) tenure
  (d) tenant
7 (a) primary   primitive
     prime   primeval
     premier
  (b) Important. A primate has an important job in the church because he is the first or chief person in the church.
  (c) The root of the word "premier" tells me that the premier is the first or most important person in parliament.
8 (a) benefit
  (b) benefactor
  (c) benevolent
  (d) benediction
9 (a) autograph: a signature (a written name)
  (b) telegraph: a method of sending and receiving messages
  (c) paragraph: a section of writing (in a composition, for example)
  (d) biography: the story of a person's life
  (e) graph: a line drawn to compare one value with another
10 (a) grateful: thankful
   (b) gratify: to give pleasure to, to satisfy
   (c) gratitude: showing that one is appreciated
   (d) gratuity: a donation or a tip for work done

Quiz (page 9)
1 (a) The root of "grateful" is *gratus*.
  (b) gratuity
  (c) gratify

2 (a) The root of "thermal" is *therme*.
   (b) thermostat
   (c) thermophysics
3. equestrian

2 Syllables (page 12)

Pre-test

1. sit   2. sit/ting   3. phone   4. tel/e/phone
5. Feb/ru/a/ry   6. man/u/fac/ture   7. re/mark
8. punc/tu/a/tion   9. nec/es/sar/y   10. in/de/pen/dent

Exercises

1. (a) man/ner   (c) ap/point   (e) al/so   (g) lad/der
   (b) pen/cil   (d) at/tend   (f) mo/tor   (h) lo/cal
2. no/tice, lo/tion, ro/bot, ru/ler
3. poker, silent, time, sober
4. mā/jor, kīnd, frē/quent, grāpe, mē/dium, platitūde, chīld, tūba, cūbe, cō/conut
5. lā/bour
6. (a) in/stru/ment   (b) mis/chie/vous
        mas/sa/cre   dis/ap/point
        mul/ti/ply   sep/a/rate
        dis/ap/pear   res/taur/ant
7. ex cel lent, mag a zine, oc ca sion, su per in ten dent, priv i lege (You should have the same number of syllables.)
8. rot/ten, hop/ping, com/merce, mag/net, dis/tance
9. chat/ter   fuss/ing   hit/ting   fuzz/y
   lap/ping   drop/ping   swim/mer   pain/ter
10. af/fect   aw/ful   ath/lete   e/late
    dis/patch   call/ing   har/ass   emp/ty
    sit/ting   tell/ing   tap/ping   fall/ing
11. but/ton   hum/ble
    ban/ner   pi/rate
    ra/di/o   ho/ly
    pal/ace   no/tice
    pi/lot   con/cen/trate
12. ro/ta/tion   lit/er/ate
    in/ter/rupt   sep/a/rate
    mul/ti/pli/ca/tion   ac/com/mo/da/tion
    lo/co/mo/tive   suc/cess/ful
    pop/u/lar   ben/e/fit

3 Plurals (page 23)

Pre-test

1. allies	2. buses	3. columns	4. addresses
5. classes	6. enquiries	7. universities	8. monkeys
9. studies	10. tragedies		

Exercises

1 (a) chimneys
  (b) parties
  (c) countries
  (d) donkeys
  (e) copies
  (f) journeys

2 (a) theatres
  (b) countries
  (c) tragedies
  (d) taxes
  (e) columns
  (f) studies
  (g) buses
  (h) addresses

3 (a) enquiries
  (b) universities
  (c) valleys
  (d) surveys
  (e) properties
  (f) dresses
  (g) pitches
  (h) replies

4 (a) taxes
  (b) buses
  (c) bungalows
  (d) arches
  (e) addresses
  (f) columns

5 (a) surveys
  (b) replies
  (c) theatres
  (d) watches
  (e) dairies

6 (a) parties
  (b) tragedies
  (c) enquiries
  (d) counties
  (e) societies
  (f) universities
  (g) studles
  (h) properties
  (i) countries

7 (a) discoveries
  (b) chimneys
  (c) worries

4 More difficult plurals (page 29)

Pre-test

1. halves	2. tomatoes	3. knives	4. radios
5. potatoes	6. solos	7. pianos	8. leaves
9. heroes	10. shelves		

Exercises

1. echoes   mosquitoes   piccolos   Negroes
   solos   tomatoes   heroes   vetoes

2. knives   lives   loaves   shelves   thieves
   wives   selves   leaves   calves   halves

3 (a) zoos
   (b) tomatoes
   (c) shelves
   (d) yourselves
   (e) leaves
   (f) wives
   (g) mosquitoes
   (h) thieves

4 (a) knives
   (b) calves
   (c) echoes
   (d) potatoes
   (e) embargoes
   (f) halves
   (g) mottoes
   (h) solos

5 (a) thieves
   (b) knives
   (c) zoos
   (d) mosquitoes
   (e) potatoes, tomatoes
   (f) pianos, banjos, sopranos, contraltos, solos

6 (a) heroes
   (b) roofs
   (c) Negroes
   (d) cargoes
   (e) leaves
   (f) pianos

7 (a) wolves   (c) shelves   (e) leaves
   (b) halves   (d) thieves   (f) yourselves

8 (a) tomato   (c) Negro   (e) piano
   (b) potato   (d) radio   (f) photo

9 (a) solos   (d) addresses
   (b) vetoes   (e) radios
   (c) enquiries   (f) loaves

5 Homonyms (page 38)

Pre-test

1. passed 2. coarse 3. their 4. practice
5. formally 6. principles 7. loose 8. all together
9. it's 10. stationery

Exercises

1
(a) stationary
(b) altogether
(c) past
(d) compliment
(e) their
(f) alter
(g) formerly
(h) loose
(i) practice
(j) weather
(k) principal
(l) course

2
(a) altar
(b) stationery
(c) principle
(d) all together
(e) passed
(f) coarse
(g) complement
(h) there
(i) formally
(j) lose
(k) practise
(l) whether

3
(a) practice
(b) past
(c) passed
(d) practise
(e) advice
(f) past

6 Double letters (page 45)

Pre-test

1. commission
2. accommodation
3. oppose
4. occasion
5. necessary
6. until
7. success
8. skilful
9. harass
10. occurred

Exercises
1 (a) paral<u>l</u>el   (f) ac<u>c</u>ount
  (b) quar<u>r</u>el   (g) ac<u>c</u>use
  (c) su<u>cces</u>s   (h) omi<u>tt</u>ed
  (d) a<u>cce</u>ss   (i) tra<u>ff</u>ic
  (e) begi<u>nn</u>ing   (j) o<u>ccur</u>red
2 (a) accuse: to charge with wrong-doing
  (b) account: a record or a reckoning
  (c) accost: to speak to a stranger in a familiar or rude way
  (d) accouchement: the childbirth period
  (e) accomplish: to achieve something
  (f) accompany: to go with a person
  (g) accommodation: somewhere to live
  (h) acclimatise: to become used to a climate
  (i) accelerate: to increase speed
  (j) accumulate: to collect or increase

7   Word endings — "ly" and "ally" (page 52)

Pre-test
1. critically   2. usually   3. automatically   4. entirely
5. sensibly   6. certainly   7. apologetically   8. probably
9. reliably   10. accidentally

Exercises
1. equally   2. sincerely
  critically   sensibly
  academically   simply
  naturally   rarely
3 (a) noisily   messily   (b) weary   lazy
      easily   happily   crazy   wary
4 (a) automatically (ic)   5 (a) fundamentally (ly)
  (b) usually (ly)   (b) morally (ly)
  (c) publicly (exception)   (c) severely (ly)
  (d) sensibly (ly)   (d) apologetically (ic)
  (e) entirely (ly)   (e) equally (ly)
  (f) drastically (ic)   (f) simply (ly)
  (g) basically (ic)   (g) easily (ly)
  (h) critically (ic)   (h) cruelly (ly)
  (i) probably (ly)   (i) reliably (ly)
  (j) certainly (ly)   (j) accidentally (ly)

6 (a) usually
   (b) publicly
   (c) probably
   (d) sensibly
   (e) entirely

   (f) automatically
   (g) critically
   (h) basically
   (i) drastically
   (j) apologetically

7. *"ally"*
   apologetically
   automatically
   basically
   critically
   drastically

   "ly"
   usually
   probably
   severely
   entirely
   sensibly
   publicly
   permanently

8 (a) cruelly
   (b) simply
   (c) morally
   (d) easily
   (e) equally

9. automatically
   publicly
   certainly

   drastically
   reliably
   accidentally

8 Which to use — "ei" or "ie"? (page 58)

Pre-test

1. chief   2. weight   3. foreign   4. believe
5. niece   6. piece   7. yield   8. ceiling
9. conceit   10. freight

Exercises

1. believe   relieve   niece   grievance   brief
   piece   field   handkerchief   chief   retrieve
   ("Either" may also be pronounced with an "ee" sound.)
   When the sound is "ee" write "i" before "e".

2. *"ei"*
   receive
   conceive
   deceit
   receipt

   "ie"
   yield
   retrieve
   shriek
   believe
   field
   relief

141

When the sound is "ee", write "i" before "e" except after "c".

3. belief   weight
   receive   perceive
   deceit   ceiling
   vein   foreign
   niece   grief
4. weight (Example (c))
   relief (Example (a))
   piece (Example (a))
   receipt (Example (b))
   freight (Example (c))
   believe (Example (a))
5. (a) deceive   6 (a) grievance
   (b) chief   (b) shriek
   (c) foreign   (c) leisure
   (d) freight   (d) believe
   (e) ceiling   (e) alien
   (f) niece   (f) brief
   (g) height   (g) forfeit
   (h) weight   (h) perceive
   (i) relief   (i) receive
   (j) conceit   (j) neighbour
7. (a) deceive
   (b) conceit
   (c) receive
   (d) niece
   (e) neighbours
   (f) relieve
   (g) believe
8. "ei"   "ie"
   freight   piece
   leisure   relief
   foreign   belief
   weight   chief
   eight
   receive
   height
   forfeit
9. grievance, conceivable, cashier, thief, siege

9 Word endings — "eous", "ious" and "ous" (page 68)

Pre-test

1. dangerous　2. courageous　3. various　4. gracious
5. vigorous　6. outrageous　7. delicious　8. mischievous
9. conscious　10. humorous

Exercises

1. (a) courageous
   (b) mysterious
   (c) ridiculous
   (d) mischievous
   (e) outrageous
   (f) gracious
   (g) spacious
   (h) various
   (i) dangerous
   (j) grievous

2. (a) delicious
   (b) obvious
   (c) serious
   (d) plenteous
   (e) obnoxious
   (f) ferocious
   (g) religious
   (h) conscious
   (i) mountainous
   (j) advantageous

3. *"eous"*
   courageous
   advantageous
   bounteous
   gorgeous
   piteous
   outrageous
   plenteous

   "ious"
   obvious
   mysterious
   ferocious
   various
   religious
   spacious
   conscious
   obnoxious

4. spacious
   courageous
   grievous
   dangerous
   ridiculous

   outrageous
   mysterious
   various
   mischievous
   gracious

5. (a) spacious
   (b) delicious
   (c) obnoxious
   (d) outrageous
   (e) obvious
   (f) various

6. mischievous　mountainous　gracious
   ridiculous　grievous　obvious
   courageous　dangerous　religious

143

7 (a) gracious
  (b) abstemious
  (c) devious
  (d) studious
  (e) various
  (f) previous
  (g) serious

10 Long and short vowel sounds (page 74)

Pre-test

1. writing	2. hopping	3. pinned	4. canned
5. ripen	6. planed	7. written	8. fitter
9. banned	10. ripped		

Exercises

1. tāme   rīpe   rōpe   clīmb   bē
2. căp   cāpe   răt   rāte   hŏp
   hōpe   slīde   slĭd   ūse   ŭs
   rŏb   rōbe   fīne   fĭn   pāne
   păn   făt   fāte   strīpe   strip
3. wrīting   hōping   pīning   pĭnning
   rōbing   rŏbbing   cănning   cāning
4. pinning, robbing, padding, ripping, slapping
5 (a) writing, sliding, grating, hoping, gaping, claiming
  (b) grated, hoped, gaped, claimed
6 (a) naming   letting   betting   thinning   spinning
      throwing   biting   sagging   planing   staining
  (b) rammed   creamed   mailed   rubbed   cropped
      slipped   feared   coated   seated   jailed

11 Silent letters (page 80)

Pre-test

1. autumn	2. undoubtedly	3. gnawed	4. rheumatism
5. eight	6. exhaust	7. whole	8. known
9. descend	10. condemn		

Exercises

1 (a) debt   (f) psychologist
  (b) rhythm   (g) know
  (c) fasten   (h) hours
  (d) doubt   (i) autumn
  (e) writer   (j) shepherd

2 (a) condemn   (f) gnomes
  (b) descend   (g) ghost
  (c) exhausted   (h) weigh
  (d) subtle   (i) whether
  (e) Wednesday   (j) would
3. brought   debt   rheumatism
  descend   fasten   shepherd
  rhythm   exhausted   autumn
  condemn   whether   ghost
  hours   gnome   writer
4 (a) debt
  (b) Wednesday
  (c) doubt
  (d) descend
  (e) fasten
5 (a) known   (d) subtle
  (b) rhythm   (e) debt
  (c) exhaust   (f) writer
6 (a) It is not known whether the debt will be repaid by Wednes-
     day.
  (b) The condemned man was undoubtedly guilty.
  (c) The writer worked such long hours that he was exhausted.
  (d) It was a subtle move but I did not doubt that it would suc-
     ceed.
  (e) She was advised to weigh the advisability or otherwise of
     consulting a psychiatrist.

12   Words with "ph" (page 86)

Pre-test
1. telephone   2. pamphlet   3. fantastic   4. blaspheme
5. prophet   6. phantom   7. autobiography   8. stupefy
9. nephews   10. orphan
Exercises
1 (a) telephone
  (b) pharmacist
  (c) phenomenon
  (d) phantom
  (e) physical
  (f) physics

2 (a) prophecy
(b) prophesy
(c) prophecy
3. fantasy, physique, fallacy, blaspheme, pamphlet, falcon
4 (a) microphone
(b) phrase
(c) symphony
(d) phonograph
5 (a) physique
(b) physics
(c) physician
(d) physical
(e) physiology

6. emphatic   telegraph   pamphlet
   photograph   physique   blaspheme
   orphan   physician   phobia

13   Consonants before "ed" (page 92)

Pre-test

1. offered   6. benefited
2. happened   7. committed
3. visited   8. buttered
4. panicked   9. preferred
5. picnicked   10. permitted

Exercises

1 (b) benefited equipped differed
      ordered   admitted referred
      permitted offered   opened
      occurred   visited   omitted

2 (a) offered
  (b) regretted
  (c) visited
  (d) happened
  (e) permitted
  (f) benefited
  (g) trafficked
  (h) referred

3 (a) begin   commit   benefit   toboggan
      gallop   refer   occur   prefer

146

(b) beginning   committing   benefiting   tobogganing
    galloping   referring   occurring   preferring

14   Word endings — "cede", "ceed" and "sede" (page 96)

Pre-test

1. succeed
2. supersede
3. proceed
4. concede

5. exceed
6. intercede
7. precede
8. recede

Exercises

1. "ceed"

2 (a) intercede
  (b) concede
  (c) proceed
  (d) supersede
  (e) precede
  (f) succeed
  (g) recede
  (h) exceed
  (i) accede

3 (a) supersede
  (b) proceed, exceed, succeed
  (c) "cede"
  (d) super
  (e) "ceed"

4 (a) supersede
  (b) proceed
  (c) exceed
  (d) succeed

5 (a) succeed
  (b) recede
  (c) proceed
  (d) supersede
  (e) intercede
  (f) accede

6 (a) intercede
  (b) "ceed"
  (c) exceed
  (d) concede
  (e) "sede" (or "s")
  (f) "cede"
  (g) proceed
  (h) accede

15 Word endings — "able" and "ible" (page 103)

Pre-test

1. inflexible
2. unseasonable
3. incredible
4. perishable
5. incurable
6. debatable
7. permissible
8. edible
9. available
10. divisible

Exercises

1 (a) respectable
  (b) remarkable
  (c) noticeable
  (d) horrible
  (e) suitable
  (f) profitable
  (g) favourable

2. terrible   manageable
   workable   audible
   enjoyable   fashionable
   possible   plausible

3. agreeable   workable   peaceable
   incredible   permissible   pronounceable
   perishable   divisible   uncontrollable

16 Prefixes — to double or not? (page 108)

Pre-test

1. misbehave
2. disappear
3. misspelling
4. unnecessary
5. untangle
6. immigrants
7. miscalculated
8. misspent
9. irreversible
10. dissatisfied

Exercises

1 (a) misjudge: to judge wrongly
      misconduct: wrong conduct
      miscalculate: to calculate wrongly
      misadventure: an accidental happening
      misbehave: to behave badly
      mismanage: to manage badly
  (b) Misspell. The ''s'' is written twice because the base word begins with ''s''.
  (c) misspent: badly spent
      misshaped: badly shaped
      misprint: mistake in printing

The first two words contain double "s" because the base word begins with "s".

2 (a) disappoint: not to do what was expected

disappear: not appear (to vanish)

The "s" is written once because the base word does not begin with "s".

(b) dissatisfied: not satisfied

disservice: of no service or help, an action that causes harm

dissimilar: not similar

3 (a) unnatural

(b) twice

(c) The "n" occurred at the end of the prefix and again at the beginning of the base word.

4 (a) impossible   (e) implausible

(b) impersonal   (f) immoral

(c) immature   (g) immense

(d) imprison

5. irrecoverable, irrational, irresponsible, irreversible, irregular

The ladders of success

Complete the appropriate ladder to show how many words you spelt correctly, e.g., if you spelt nine words correctly on the Pre-test, shade the ladder from 1 to 9.

Write the misspelt words at the side of the ladder in the space provided. N.B. This page only is free of copyright and may therefore be copied by any means.

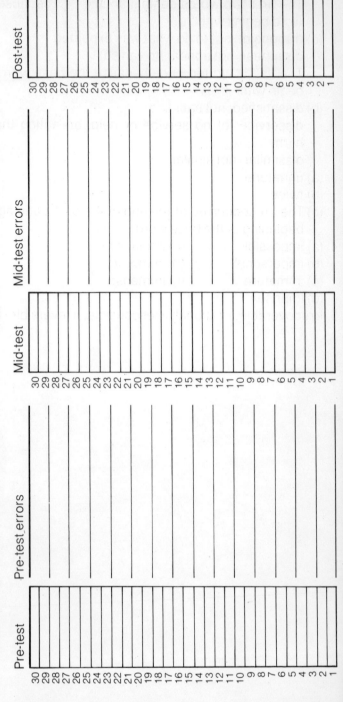

Pre-test

Pre-test errors

Mid-test

Mid-test errors

Post-test